C000261499

25 YEARS OF MOTOR CRUISERS

Other titles in the *Motorboats Monthly* series

Starting Motorboating: Emrhys Barrell
Practical Motor Cruising: Dag Pike
Fast Boats and Rough Seas: Dag Pike
Fast Boat Navigation: Dag Pike
Marine Inboard Engines: Loris Goring
The Outboard Motor Manual: Keith Henderson

If you are interested in any of the above titles contact:
Adlard Coles Nautical
35 Bedford Row,
London WC1R 4JH
or
Motorboats Monthly at
Link House,
Dingwall Avenue,
Croydon,
Surrey CR9 2TA.

25 YEARS OF MOTOR CRUISERS

1960-1984

Alex McMullen

ADLARD COLES NAUTICAL

London

Published by Adlard Coles Nautical
an imprint of
A & C Black (Publishers) Ltd
35 Bedford Row,
London WC1R 4JH.

Copyright © Alex McMullen 1991

First published in Great Britain by Adlard Coles Nautical 1991

ISBN 0–7136–3459–6

Apart from any fair dealing for the purpose of research or private study, or criticism or review, as permitted under the Copyright, Designs and Patents Act, 1988, this publication may be reproduced, stored or transmitted, in any forms or by any means, only with the prior permission in writing of the publishers, or in the case of reprographic reproduction in accordance with the terms of licences issued by the Copyright Licensing Agency. Inquiries concerning reproduction outside those terms should be sent to the publishers at the address above.

A CIP catalogue record for this book is available from the British Library.

Printed and bound in Great Britain by Courier International, East Kilbride.

Contents

Introduction

MANY of the names in this book will be very familiar, some will jog faint memories, a few may have been forgotten. But all the boats described and illustrated here – motor cruisers from 20 ft to 45 ft in length, in production between 1960 and 1984 – are significant, either for the numbers built, or as milestones in design, or because they are already classics, much sought after in the secondhand market.

If, in 25 years' time, someone writes a book about the motor cruisers built during the period 1985 to 2009, I doubt that it will match the variety of boats included here. The 1960s, in particular, were a fascinating period in motorboat building. The era of mass production had begun, led by the likes of Freeman, Seamaster and Senior Marine, but it was still possible to buy, new, a traditional timber displacement motorboat, like a Rampart, a Bates Starcraft or a Jaunty. A number of superb fast cruisers had also emerged, like the Fairey Huntsman, the product of competition in offshore racing. In those days the Cowes–Torquay powerboat race had some relevance to the boating world at large.

In the 1970s and early '80s the volume building of motor cruisers increased dramatically, as did the sizes of boats coming off production lines. Boats such as the Princess 32 and the Moonraker 36 opened the door to production building of 40-footers and now 50- and 60-footers. This period also saw the establishment, from humble beginnings, of the various ranges of cruisers – Fairline, Princess, Birchwood, Sealine and Sunseeker – that now dominate the market.

So what will happen between now and 2009? Maybe something really new will come along in design and construction, but good as many of them are, there is a noticeable sameness amongst current cruisers.

The boats in this book are arranged in size order, but they can be located using the alphabetical index on page 183. For each we give the following details: dimensions (length overall, beam, draught) and construction material; builders, numbers of boats built and period of production; particular features of the boat and its history; accommodation layout; hull design; and engines and top speeds. In the case of some of the older boats, speeds may be theoretical – in other words boat and engine(s) may not be able to achieve what they once could.

Acknowledgements

Thanks are due above all to Kim Hollamby, Editor of *Motorboats Monthly*, for publishing the series on which this book is based. Thanks also to Myrna White for her meticulous work in producing all the profile and plan drawings; to Patrick Kelley, former Art Editor of *Motorboats Monthly*, for designing the boat entries and for much help in producing the references for the drawings; to Janet Evans and Guy Thomas for their editing and proof reading; and to Stuart Reed of South-West Graphics, who carried out all the setting and film-making of the boat entries.

A great many people helped me in my researches. Paul Wagstaffe, Chief Executive of the British Marine Industries Federation, gave invaluable assistance in providing material on a number of boats. I would also like to thank the following for the information they gave me and for the time that I know many of them spent delving through their archives for details of boats and illustrations: Steve Adams, Diana Bates, John Bennett, David Beresford, Justin Birt, Bob Braithwaite, Ted Breeze, David Bromley, Peter Brown, Tim Bulmer, Bill Buxton, Graham Caddick, Derek Chapman, Wallace Clark, Charles Clarke, Andrew Constance, Len Cox, John Desty, Roy Dutfield, Barbara Edney, David Freeman, Peter Geoffrey, Paul Hadley, Peter Hansford, Chris Harridge, Bill Harrison, Dave Houghton, Mary Instance, Robert Kemp, Sidney Latimer, Ann Leeson, Bob Love, Ralph Lovell, Bill Maloney, John Moxham, Rosemary Mudie, Arthur Mursell, Briony Newington, Pat Noyes, Brian Peters, Jacqueline Phillipson, George Pittock, Robin Poulton, Eddy Rawle, Bernie Reinman, Ian Robinson, Denys Sessions, Richard Shead, Sam Sims, Alan Taylor, Bob Tough, Geoff Townley, Anthony Trafford, Diana Tremlett, Richard Trevor, Colin Watts, Ernie Whealdon and Graham Whealdon.

Alex McMullen

vii

DOLPHIN 20

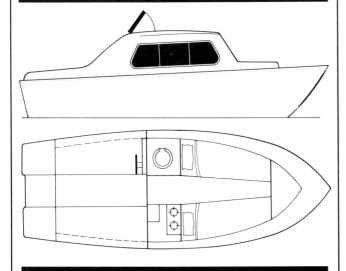

IN the 1960s and early '70s Brooklands Aviation (the company started life in the aircraft industry) introduced thousands of people to motor boating with their Dolphin range of dayboats and small cruisers. They built just under 700 Dolphin 20s between 1962 and 1974. The first 600 were built of marine ply, but a MkII version was introduced in 1972 with GRP hull and ply superstructure. The boats were popular on rivers and in estuarial and sheltered coastal waters.

There is accommodation for two in the cabin, which has a galley and a separate toilet compartment, with two settees in the cockpit which can be used as occasional berths under the cockpit canopy.

Hull shape is shallow to medium vee. A few boats were fitted with outdrive petrol engines, such as the 80hp Mangoletsi Ford, but the vast majority are outboard powered. The favoured size was 40hp but for river use 15hp would be quite enough. Some owners have installed twin outboards, up to 40hp each. A single 40hp outboard should give a top speed of about 18 to 22 knots, depending on load; with two 40s, or the 80hp Mangoletsi, the boat should reach 25 to 28 knots.

Length overall	20ft 0in (6.10m)
Beam	6ft 10in (2.08m)
Draught	10in (0.25m)
Hull/deck material	wood or GRP/wood

DRACO 2000

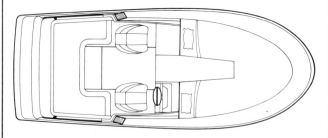

Length overall	20ft 0in (6.10m)
Beam	7ft 7in (2.31m)
Draught	2ft 6in (0.76m)
Hull/deck material	GRP

DESIGNED by Jan Linge, who also designed the Soling Olympic keelboat, and built by Draco AS of Norway, the Draco 2000 Daycab Sportling was launched in 1967. From 1970 until 1984 over 800 were imported into the UK, Dell Quay Sales being the original agents, followed by Northshore Yacht Yards and B A Peters & Partners.

The boat is suitable for day or weekend boating, with a large cockpit and a very basic cabin under the foredeck — two berths, a toilet between the berths and space for a small cooker.

The boat's deep-vee simulated clinker hull is driven by a single outdrive engine, most commonly a 130hp petrol Volvo, giving a top speed of over 25 knots. In the 1973 Cowes-Torquay powerboat race a Draco 2000, powered by a 170hp Volvo petrol engine, finished a creditable 15th, at an average speed of 29 knots.

HARDY FAMILY PILOT

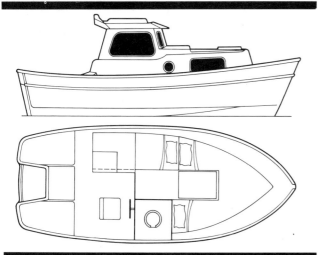

DESIGNED BY Colin Mudie and built by Hardy Marine, the Hardy Family Pilot was launched in 1980 and is still in production. Over 500 have been built to date.

The boat has a largish aft cockpit, an open-backed wheelhouse which houses a galley — the wheelhouse and cockpit can be enclosed by a canopy — and a cabin with three berths and separate toilet compartment. The sunken side decks — or raised topsides — are an unusual (and attractive) feature on such a small boat.

At first glance the hull looks like a traditional round-bilge displacement form, but from midships aft the underwater sections are shallow-vee, allowing full planing performance, while a long shallow keel aids handling at low speeds. With an outboard engine of the recommended maximum 70hp, top speed is between 17 and 20 knots, depending on load.

Length overall	20ft 0in (6.10m)
Beam	8ft 0in (2.44m)
Draught	2ft 0in (0.61m)
Hull/deck material	GRP

SEAMASTER 20

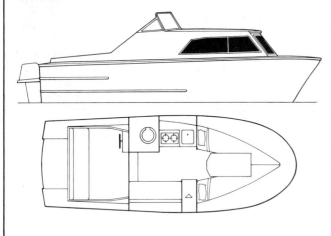

SEAMASTER Ltd of Great Dunmow, Essex, were once one of the most prolific builders of GRP motor cruisers, producing about 3000 boats from the mid-1950s through the '60s and '70s. The Seamaster 20 was launched in 1964 and 165 were built up to 1975, most of them for river use though the boat is suitable for estuarial and sheltered coastal waters in fair weather.

An open-plan cabin has three berths, with a galley, and there is a separate toilet compartment.

Hull shape is basically round-bilge but with flattish underwater sections aft. Most boats were fitted with a Ford petrol inboard of 40 to 60hp, giving a top speed of about 10 knots, but some are outboard-powered, the maximum recommended power being 50hp, which would drive the boat at up to about 18 knots.

Length overall	20ft 0in (6.10m)
Beam	7ft 4in (2.23m)
Draught	1ft 8in (0.51m)
Hull/deck material	GRP

NORMAN 20

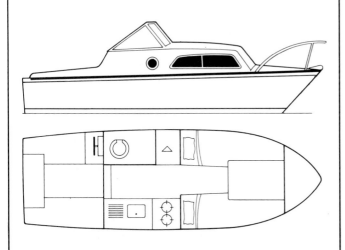

THE Norman 20 was one of the most popular small cruisers of the 1970s. Norman Cruisers, of Shaw, Lancashire, built over 1000 of them between 1971 and 1980. They are usually seen on inland waterways but they were sold as seagoing craft and are capable of undertaking short fair-weather passages in estuarial and sheltered coastal waters.

The boat sleeps two in the cabin, which has a separate toilet compartment, and two more can sleep in the cockpit, with the full cockpit canopy in place.

Hull shape is medium-vee with a long shallow keel. Most are powered by a single outboard engine, up to a maximum of 80hp, which would give a top speed of over 20 knots. For inland use 15 to 20hp is quite sufficient; for tidal waters, 35 to 50hp. Some boats were fitted with a petrol outdrive, typically a 90hp Ford Watermota, giving up to 24 knots.

Length overall	20ft 3in (6.17m)
Beam	6ft 10in (2.08m)
Draught	1ft 10in (0.56m)
Hull/deck material	GRP

FAIRLINE 20 FAMILY

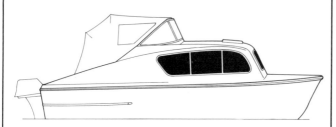

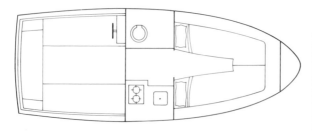

Length overall	20ft 3in (6.17m)
Beam	6ft 10in (2.08m)
Draught	9in (0.23m)
Hull/deck material	GRP

A SLIGHTLY enlarged version of the 19-footer which, in 1967, launched the now extensive range of Fairline cruisers, the Fairline 20 Family was introduced in 1972. Fairline Boats of Oundle, Northamptonshire turned out 183 of them during a three-year production period. Used primarily on rivers and canals, the boat is nonetheless capable of fair-weather trips onto estuarial or sheltered coastal waters.

There are two berths in the cabin, with a small galley and a minute toilet compartment. Seating in the cockpit can be used as two extra berths, under the cockpit canopy.

Hull shape is medium- to shallow-vee, with a long very shallow keel. The standard boat was built for outboard power, taking an engine up to 65hp, which would give a top speed of about 20 knots. Some were fitted with Volvo petrol outdrives, from 25hp, which would be quite sufficient for inland cruising at 6 or 7 knots, up to 115hp, which would drive the boat at nearly 30 knots — and require skilled handling.

SHETLAND 610 & 2+2

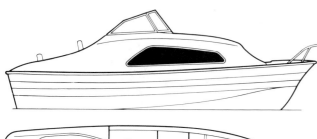

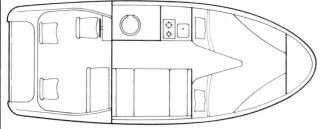

Length overall	20ft 3in (6.17m)
Beam	8ft 0in (2.44m)
Draught	1ft 6in (0.46m)
Hull/deck material	GRP

THREESTOKES (Riverside) Ltd launched the Shetland 610 in 1969. Shetland Boats took over the production in 1972 and continued to build the boat until 1974. Altogether, 385 were built. The Shetland 2+2 is a development of the 610, with a different superstructure and interior layout. It was launched in 1970 and about 200 were built up to 1974. The photograph and drawings are of the 610.

Both boats have two vee berths forward; the 610 also has a dinette which converts to a double berth, while the 2+2 has a double berth under the forward, raised part of the cockpit. The 610 has space for a small galley and chemical toilet, while the 2+2 has a fitted galley and small toilet compartment. The 2+2's higher superstructure also provides a limited area of full headroom in the cabin.

Colin Mudie designed the boats, giving them a simulated-clinker hull with a deep-vee bottom. They can be powered by single outboard engines of up to 120hp, which should give a top speed of over 30 knots. A few 610s and about fifty 2+2s were fitted with petrol outdrive engines of various makes and powers.

SHETLAND SPEEDWELL

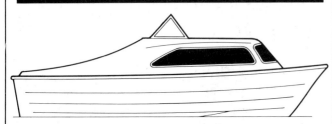

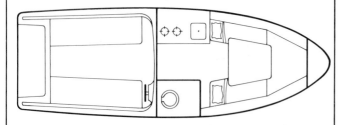

Length overall	20ft 3in (6.17m)
Beam	6ft 10in (2.08m)
Draught	1ft 6in (0.46m)
Hull/deck material	GRP

SIMILAR at first glance to the Shetland 610, with a Colin Mudie-designed, simulated-clinker hull of exactly the same length, the Shetland Speedwell is, in fact, considerably narrower in the beam. It was designed for cruising on the narrow canals as well as on rivers and on sheltered estuarial and coastal waters, in fair weather. Shetland Boats built 411 Speedwells between 1970 and 1974.

There are two berths in the cabin, with a simple galley and separate toilet compartment. The seats in the cockpit can be converted into occasional berths, under a canopy.

The boat can be powered by a single outboard of up to 70hp (in experienced hands), giving a top speed of about 25 knots, but for inland use a 9hp long-shaft outboard would be quite sufficient.

TOD TUNA

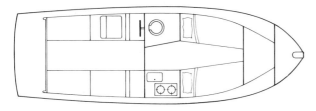

Length overall	20ft 5in (6.22m)
Beam	6ft 11in (2.11m)
Draught	2ft 0in (0.61m)
Hull/deck material	GRP

IN the motorboating hall of fame there should be a prominent place for the Tod Tuna as it was the first GRP production motorboat. The model dates back to 1954, but remained in production until 1970. W & J Tod of Weymouth built about 300 Tunas during that time.

The boat has a basic cabin with two berths, a toilet and space for a small galley. On a few boats the open cockpit was partially covered by a hardtop.

Hull shape is shallow-vee with two small bilge keels. A variety of engines were fitted over the years, including single petrol and diesel inboards and outdrives, two inboard petrol engines and single or twin outboards. Most of the earliest boats were powered by twin 30hp Ford Watermota petrol inboards, later models by 50hp Watermotas or 60hp Volvo petrol engines. With two 50hp Watermotas the boat should achieve 22 knots, and with two 60hp Volvos 26 to 28 knots.

DOMINATOR

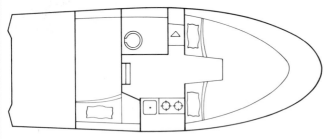

THE Dominator high-speed outboard cruiser, designed by John Bennett, was launched in 1972 by FAME Ltd. The boat was also built, in later years, by Florence Marine and then by Picton Boats who bought the moulds in 1978, and renamed it the **Picton 210 Fiesta Four.** About 300 Dominators and nearly 300 Fiesta Fours have been built.

The boat sleeps four — two forward and two under the raised helm position — and has a separate toilet compartment.

The medium-vee hull was designed to be powered by one or two outboards up to a total of 100hp. With 85hp, which is probably a sensible maximum for most owners, top speed would be about 30 knots. A few Dominators and Fiesta Fours have been fitted with single petrol outdrives.

Length overall	21ft 0in (6.40m)
Beam	8ft 0in (2.44m)
Draught	2ft 0in (0.61m)
Hull/deck material	GRP

PACEMAKER 21

PORT Hamble launched the first Pacemaker 21 in 1962 and during the next three years built between 30-40, which in those days was a fair number. This high-speed sports cruiser was built of marine ply. The medium to deep-vee bottom was made up of broad reverse-clinker 'planks' of ply, thus providing built-in spray rails. Pacemaker 21s competed in — and completed — the 1962 and 1963 Cowes-Torquay Powerboat Races.

The boat has two berths, a galley and a separate, if rather small, toilet compartment.

Power comes from single or twin petrol outdrives. The two race boats were fitted with twin 110hp Volvos giving a top speed of over 35 knots.

Length overall	21ft 0in (6.40m)
Beam	8ft 3in (2.51m)
Draught	2ft 7in (0.79m)
Hull/deck material	wood

RELCRAFT 21 PEARL

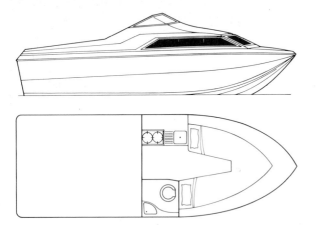

RELIANCE Marine introduced the Relcraft 650 Pearl sports cruiser at the 1982 London Boat Show, and built between 70 and 80 up to 1986.

The boat sleeps two in a small cabin which has a galley and a separate toilet compartment. Nearly half the length of the boat is taken up with a large aft cockpit.

John Moxham designed the Pearl (and all the other boats in the Relcraft range), giving it a deep vee hull with large concave chines which effectively act as sponsons, increasing lift and stability. Single petrol outdrive engines of various makes (mostly Volvos, but Mercruisers and BMWs too) have been fitted, of powers ranging from 120 to 230hp, although Reliance recommended a maximum 185hp, which should give 28-knot performance.

Length overall	21ft 0in (6.40m)
Beam	7ft 10in (2.39m)
Draught	2ft 0in (0.61m)
Hull/deck material	GRP

SHETLAND 640

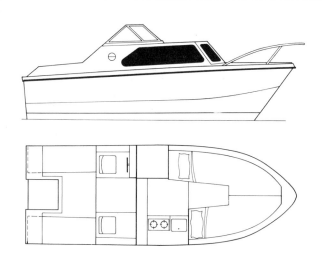

Length overall	21ft 0in (6.40m)
Beam	8ft 6in (2.59m)
Draught	2ft 0in (0.61m)
Hull/deck material	GRP

DESIGNED for river and fair-weather coastal cruising, the Shetland 640 was in production from 1972 to 1978. Shetland Boats (now Shetland Cruisers) built about 400 640s during that period.

The cabin has two berths, a galley and separate toilet compartment, while two seats in the cockpit can be used as occasional berths under the cockpit canopy — short singles or, with a fill-in piece, an athwartships double.

The shallow-vee hull is suitable for outboard engines up to 45hp, which would give a top speed, lightly laden, of about 18 knots, though the hull form is not really suited to such speeds in anything other than calm water. Some boats were fitted with outdrive petrol engines of various makes and powers; others have been subsequently modified.

SORCERER 21

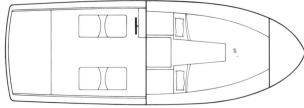

Length overall	21ft 0in (6.40m)
Beam	7ft 0in (2.13m)
Draught	2ft 0in (0.61m)
Hull/deck material	GRP

DESIGNER Bill Maloney based the Sorcerer 21 on the same lines as his 21ft powerboat *Bewitched*, a successful Class III offshore racer which beat many larger boats in finishing a remarkable sixth overall in the 1967 Cowes-Torquay Race. David Harber (Barlaston) built about 35 Sorcerer 21s, between 1967 and 1970.

The boat has a large cockpit and a small cabin with basic accommodation — two vee-berths and a toilet under the connecting foot end, with space also for a mini galley.

In common with Maloney's other powerboat designs, the hull shape is semi deep-vee (deep-vee at midships, medium-vee aft) with slightly concave sections and distinctly large sprayrails (to help provide lift, not just to deflect spray). Power comes from a single petrol outdrive engine, the most popular of which was a 140hp Mercruiser which would drive the boat at up to 30 knots.

TREMLETT SPORTSMAN 21

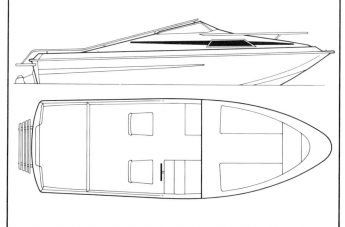

Length overall	21ft 0in (6.40m)
Beam	7ft 6in (2.29m)
Draught	2ft 3in (0.69m)
Hull/deck material	GRP

BASED on the same deep-vee hull as their successful hot-moulded timber racing boats from the late 1960s, the 21 Sportsman was launched by Tremlett Boat Sales of Topsham, Devon, in 1970. The boat is still in production, more than 400 having been built to date.

Over half the length of the boat is taken up by cockpit, the accommodation being limited to a small cabin with two berths, a toilet and space for a galley.

Some Sportsmans are outboard-powered but most have a single outdrive engine. In recent years many have been fitted with diesels, but before 1985 petrol was the norm. Early boats have 140 or 175hp Mercruisers, later ones a 145hp Volvo which enable them to achieve a modest 35 knots or so. The most powerful installation has been a 225hp Chrysler, driving the boat at nearly 45 knots.

FJORD 21 WEEKENDER

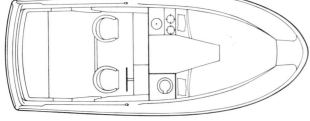

FJORD Plast of Norway introduced the Fjord 21 in 1969. In the UK at least, the Weekender was the most popular of the three versions available — other versions being the Daycruiser and Hardtop. About 100 were imported into the UK, up to 1980. The original importers, J G Meakes, called the boat the Fjord Holiday.

The Weekender/Holiday has accommodation for four, two in the main cabin and two in a mid-cabin or mini-cabin under the forward raised part of the open cockpit, Fjord having pioneered the mid-cabin in their 24 Weekender (the Daycruiser and the Hardtop have just two berths, in the Hardtop under an open-backed cuddy).

The boat was designed by Eivind Amble and has a deep-vee hull. The most common engine is a 170hp Volvo petrol outdrive, which should give a top speed approaching 30 knots.

Length overall	21ft 3in (6.48m)
Beam	8ft 2in (2.49m)
Draught	2ft 3in (0.69m)
Hull/deck material	GRP

FAIRLINE 21 WEEKEND

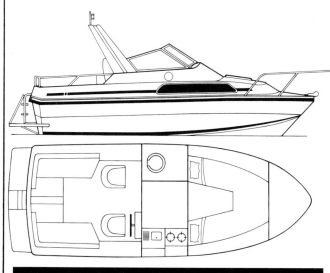

Length overall	21ft 5in (6.53m)
Beam	8ft 1in (2.46m)
Draught	2ft 8in (0.81m)
Hull/deck material	GRP

THE Fairline 21 Weekend was launched in 1979 and designed by Bernard Olesinski, who was responsible for most of the recent and all the current boats in the Fairline range. By 1987, when production ceased, 485 Weekends had emerged from the Fairline Boats factory in Oundle, Northamptonshire.

Surprisingly spacious for its length, the boat has a roomy two-berth cabin, with galley and toilet compartment, and a cockpit with driver's and navigator's seats and, around the stern, seating for five or six which can be converted into a large sunlounger or, with the cockpit canopy in place, a fair-weather double berth.

The hull is deep-vee from bow to midships, medium-vee at the stern, with a pronounced full-length chine flat — typical Olesinski. Power comes from one of a range of single petrol or diesel outdrives. A 200hp petrol Volvo, as commonly fitted, should give 30 knots or more.

NORMAN 22

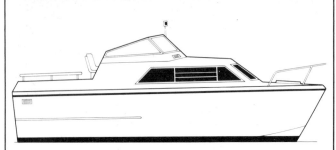

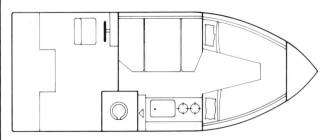

NORMAN Cruisers introduced the Norman22 in 1978 and built about 60 of them up to 1982. Some were bought primarily as river cruisers, some, with the more powerful engine options, for fast boating in estuarial and sheltered coastal waters.

The boat has four berths in an open-plan cabin, with a separate toilet compartment, and seating for four, including the driver, in the aft cockpit.

Hull shape is medium-vee. A few boats were built to take a single outboard engine but most were fitted with a single petrol outdrive, most commonly a 120hp Volvo, which would give a top speed of over 20 knots.

Length overall 21ft 9in (6.63m)
Beam 8ft 3in (2.51m)
Draught 2ft 0in (0.61m)
Hull/deck material . . . . GRP

BIRCHWOOD 22

THIS boat was originally called the Intercepter Junior and later either the Birchwood 22 or the long-winded Birchwood Intercepter Junior 22. It was launched by Birchwood Boat Co, now Birchwood Boat International, builders of nothing smaller than 31ft (9.45m), in 1970 and about 1000 were built, up to 1980.

The boat sleeps four in a conventional open-plan, dinette-and-two-vee-berths arrangement. The helm position is out in the cockpit, usually under a hardtop shelter.

Hull shape is medium-vee. Various makes and powers of single diesel or petrol outdrives were fitted, up to 170hp. A popular choice was the 130hp petrol Volvo, driving the boat at up to 23 to 25 knots.

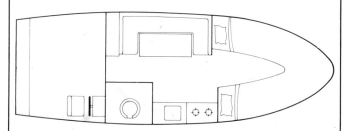

Length overall	22ft 0in (6.71m)
Beam	8ft 3in (2.51m)
Draught	2ft 0in (0.61m)
Hull/deck material	GRP

FREEMAN 22

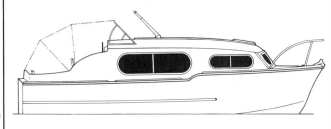

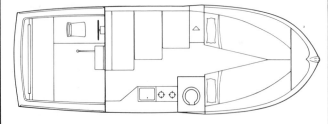

Length overall	22ft 0in (6.71m)
Beam	7ft 6in (2.29m)
Draught	2ft 0in (0.61m)
Hull/deck material	GRP

ONE of the earliest production GRP motor cruisers, the Freeman 22 was launched in 1957 by John Freeman (Marine) of Hinckley, Leicestershire. They became one of the major motor cruiser builders of the 1960s and '70s, with a reputation for smartly finished boats.

In 1964 the 22 was modified to give increased headroom forward, and a distinctive step in the deck line (as per the drawing). Over 1500 22s were built up to 1970, when the boat was superseded by the Freeman 23.

The boat has four berths in a layout which is basically open-plan but it can be divided into two cabins by opening the hanging locker door out across the boat.

Hull shape is shallow-vee with a long shallow keel. The 22 is basically a river cruiser but is capable of short estuarial or sheltered coastal passages in fair weather (Freeman's also built a narrow, 6ft 10in beam version for the canals). The boats were fitted with a 35hp Ford Watermota petrol engine or 50hp Perkins diesel, with speeds up to 9 or 10 knots.

JAUNTY 22

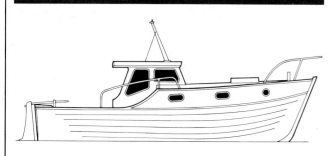

THE Jaunty 22 was first built in 1966, its larger sister the Jaunty 24 in 1967. These attractive round-bilge, displacement cruisers were designed by Peter Brown of Francis Jones & Partners. They were built (of larch or mahogany planking, clinker-laid on oak frames) by various East Coast builders, including Frank Halls of Walton-on-the-Naze, King's of Pin Mill and Everson & Sons of Woodbridge, and marketed by Beagle Boats of Woodbridge. About 30 boats of both sizes were built, up to 1971.

Both boats have a two-berth cabin under the raised foredeck, with a galley and a separate toilet compartment, an open-backed wheelhouse and a spacious aft cockpit; the difference between the two is simply in the amount of room in cabin, wheelhouse and cockpit.

Various inboard diesels were fitted — Sabb, Petter, Lister and Perkins, from 8hp to 20hp (up to 50hp in the 24), giving speeds from 6 to 8½ knots.

Illustrations are of the Jaunty 22.

	Jaunty 22	Jaunty 24
Length overall	22ft 0in (6.71m)	24ft 2in (7.37m)
Beam	8ft 4in (2.54m)	8ft 4in (2.54m)
Draught	2ft 0in (0.61m)	2ft 0in (0.61m)
Hull/deck material	wood	wood

MACLAN 22

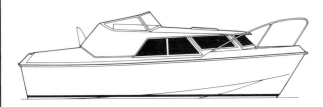

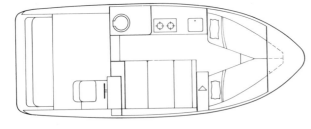

Length	22ft 0in (6.71m)
Beam	8ft 3in (2.51m)
Draught	2ft 5in (0.74m)
Hull/deck material	GRP

THE Maclan 22 was designed by Colin Mudie and about 40 of them were built by Maclan Marine between 1971 and 1975. The boat and the company were among the many victims of the imposition of 25% VAT on boats and other 'luxury' items in 1975. Only 10 of a larger version of the boat, the Maclan 25, introduced in 1973, were built. The abolition of the luxury VAT rating a year later came too late.

The Maclan 22 sleeps four — in an open-plan cabin which has two vee berths forward and a convertible dinette-cum-double berth — with a galley and a separate toilet compartment. The deep aft cockpit has seating for up to four plus the helmsman.

The boat has an unusual hull shape, medium vee on the bottom but with inverted chines — concave sections along the waterline that are designed to create a steadier motion when the boat is moving at low, displacement speed. Power comes from a single outdrive engine, most commonly a 130hp petrol BMW, which pushes the boat along at up to 24 to 25 knots.

TEAL 22

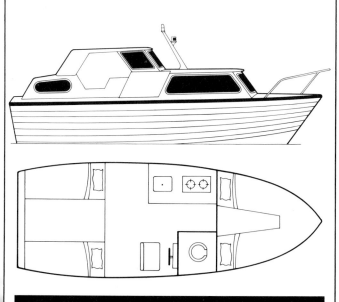

THE Teal 22, or Teal 670 as it became known towards the end of its production run, was built down to a price that made it one of the most popular small cruisers of the 1960s and early 1970s. FH Child (Marine), later Teal Marine Products, built nearly 1000 of them, between 1962 and 1973. Some boats were fitted out by other yards, such as DBH Marine of Walton-on-Thames, to a rather higher standard of finish.

There are three versions of the boat: the Convertible (illustrated), which was the most popular, has four berths in two cabins, with a centre cockpit that has a hard top and can be fully enclosed by side curtains; the Sports Fisherman has a large aft cockpit and four-berth cabin.

Hull shape is shallow-vee. Some boats were built to take an outboard engine, up to 25hp for river use, up to 100hp (and 20 knots) for (sheltered) coastal work. Some were fitted with single petrol outdrives, up to 120hp (20 to 25 knots).

Length overall	22ft 0in (6.71m)
Beam	7ft 9in (2.36m)
Draught	1ft 6in (0.46m)
Hull/deck material	GRP

WINDY 22

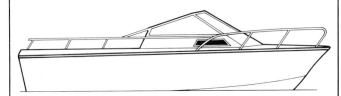

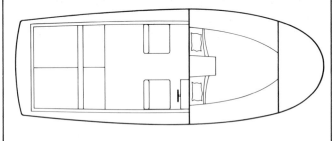

Length overall	22ft 0in (6.71m)
Beam	8ft 3in (2.51m)
Draught	2ft 11in (0.89m)
Hull/deck material	GRP

WINDY Boats of Norway built 1080 Windy 22DCs between 1967 and 1984. Designed by Jan Linge, this fast weekender was aimed at the Mediterranean market, but about 120 were imported into the UK.

The boat's huge cockpit featured a wide sunlounger across the stern — it was one of the first boats to have this now-common feature. The small cabin has two vee berths, with the option of a sea toilet under the forward mattress. A cooker could be fitted in the cockpit, under the hinged helm seat.

The 22DC has a true deep-vee hull: deadrise at the transom is 24°. It was fitted with Volvo petrol engines, in the early boats 150hp (giving a top speed of about 28 knots), and later 165hp (30 knots), 170hp (31 knots) and then 200hp (35 knots). A 260hp engine was fitted in some of the later boats, pushing top speed up to 40 knots.

WESTON 670

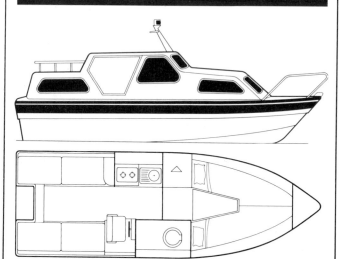

Length overall 22ft 0in (6.71m)
Beam 7ft 7in (2.31m)
Draught 1ft 7in (0.48m)
Hull/deck material .... GRP

WESTON Boats, of Colchester, Essex, have built 150 Weston 670s since 1975, and the boat is still in production. It is to be found mainly on rivers, but it is quite capable of undertaking estuarial and short coastal passages in fair weather.

The boat can sleep four or five, with two berths in a forward cabin, two in an aft cabin and a settee/berth in the midships cockpit-cum-wheelhouse — a wheelhouse with removable overhead and side canopies.

Hull shape is medium-vee with a long shallow keel. Most boats are powered by an outboard, of up to 30hp for inland use, and up to 80 or 90 for coastal work. Some have a Volvo Saildrive, of 18 or 28hp, and some owners wanting a good turn of speed have opted for a Volvo petrol outdrive of, for example, 120hp, which will drive the boat at up to 28 knots.

FAIRLINE 23 HOLIDAY

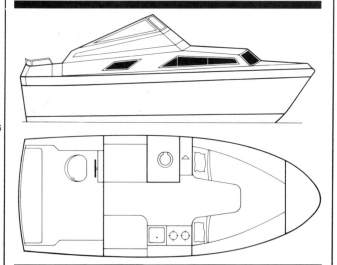

	MkI/II	MkIII
Length overall	22ft 1in (6.73m)	22ft 5in (6.83m)
Beam	8ft 6in (2.59m)	8ft 9in (2.67m)
Draught	2ft 0in (0.61m)	2ft 0in (0.61m)
Hull/deck material	GRP	GRP

MORE Fairline 23 Holidays were built than any other of Fairline Boats' range of motor cruisers, past or present. Between 1972 and 1984 a total of 594 were produced.

Despite the slight change in dimensions of the later MkIII version, all models have the same standard layout of four berths in an open-plan cabin — two single berths forward which can be converted into a double, and two single quarter-berths stretching under the cockpit. The settee across the aft end of the cockpit can be used as an occasional fifth berth, under the cockpit canopy. The photograph and drawings show a MkIII.

John Bennett designed the Holiday, which has a hull that is deep-vee back to midships but shallower and slightly rounded at the transom, with a three-quarter-length keel to impove low-speed directional stability. Various outdrive engine installations have been fitted, mostly Volvo: petrol engines from 1×125hp (giving a top speed of about 20 knots) to 2×130hp (27 to 30 knots), and single diesel engines from 60hp (12 knots) to 120hp (20-21 knots).

SEALINE 22

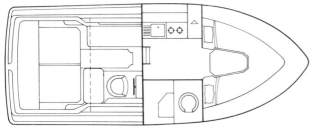

Length overall	22ft 3in (6.78m)
Beam	8ft 6in (2.59m)
Draught	2ft 6in (0.76m)
Hull/deck material	GRP

THE two versions of the Sealine 22, the Cabin and the Sport, were built by Sealine International, formerly Fibrasonic Marine. Between 1978 and 1986, when the boat was superseded by the Sealine 215, just under 300 22s were built, nearly two-thirds of them in the Sport version (as illustrated).

Both versions have four berths. The Sport, which has a much larger cockpit, has two berths in a mini-cabin under the forward, raised part of the cockpit, while the Cabin has a conventional two-vee-berths-and-convertible-dinette arrangement. Both versions have a well-equipped galley and separate toilet compartment.

The hull is deep-vee at midships, medium-vee aft. A few boats were fitted with twin petrol outdrive engines but most are powered by single outdrives, such as a 170hp Mercruiser or 175hp Volvo — both petrol — or a 165hp Volvo diesel. Top speed with any of these is in the region of 30 knots.

SUNSEEKER 23 DAYCAB

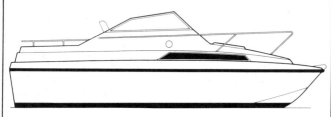

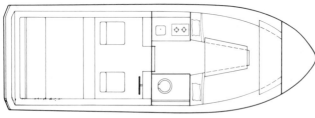

Length overall	22ft 3in (6.78m)
Beam	8ft 2in (2.49m)
Draught	2ft 9in (0.84m)
Hull/deck material	GRP

THE Sunseeker 23 Daycab sports cruiser was in production for only a couple of years, from 1977 to 1979 (when it was succeeded by the Sunseeker 235), but during that short time builders Poole Powerboats (now Sunseeker International) turned out 120 of them.

The boat sleeps four, with two berths in the main cabin and two in a mid-cabin under the forward, raised part of the large cockpit. There's a small galley and a separate toilet compartment.

Hull shape is deep-vee. Power comes from a single outdrive, commonly a 260hp Mercruiser or Volvo petrol engine, driving the boat at up to 34 to 36 knots.

CHANNEL ISLANDS 22

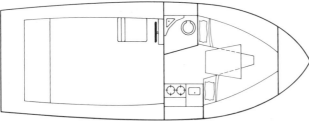

Length overall	22ft 6in (6.86m)
Beam	8ft 6in (2.62m)
Draught	2ft 6in (0.76m)
Hull/deck material	GRP

BUILT by Silva Yates (Plastics) in Guernsey, the Channel Islands 22 is a handsome round-bilge, semi-displacement motorboat designed by Alan Buchanan as both a workboat and a motor cruiser. The first CI22 was launched in 1974 and the boat is still in production, over 250 having been built.

The boat has a large aft cockpit with an open-backed wheelhouse on the same level, making it suitable for fishing. Accommodation consists of two berths with a separate toilet compartment and a galley.

Early boats were fitted with a single 72hp Ford diesel. Later examples have either a single Ford Mermaid of 135 or 155hp, the latter giving a top speed of 18 to 20 knots, or a pair of lower-powered diesels — twin 45hp BMWs, 43hp Volvos or 47hp Mermaids — which drive the boat at up to 15 or 16 knots.

CLEOPATRA 23/700

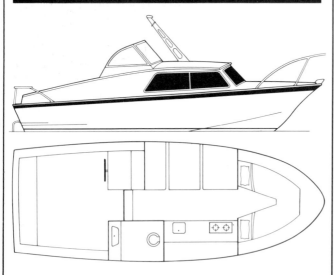

30

ESSEX Yacht Builders of Wallasea Island on the Crouch launched the Cleopatra 23 in 1967. The boat was built in two versions: Blue Nile and Express Fisherman, the latter having a larger cockpit and smaller cabin, and a hard top over the helm position.

The Blue Nile has four berths, the Express Fisherman two. In 1971 the boat was modified (one of the changes was the replacement of the rather vulnerable perspex window round the front of the cabin with two glass panels) and renamed the Cleopatra 700. Three versions of this boat were offered: the Family and the Fisherman (equivalent to the Blue Nile and Express Fisherman), and the Weekender, which had a large open cockpit and small two-berth cabin. Altogether about 400 23s and 700s were built, up to 1975. The Fox 700, built by Fox of Ipswich, was based on the same mouldings and sold in the same three versions.

Hull shape is medium-vee. Single or twin outdrive petrol engines were installed, commonly a single 50hp Perkins diesel, single 115hp or 130hp petrol Volvo, or twin 115hp Volvos, the latter giving a top speed towards 30 knots.

Length overall	22ft 9in (6.93m)
Beam	8ft 6in (2.59m)
Draught	2ft 9in (0.84m)
Hull/deck material	GRP

DRACO 2300 SUNCAB

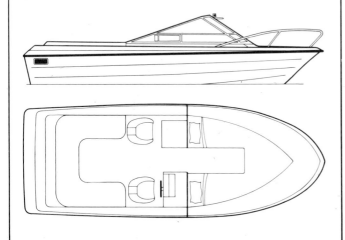

THE Draco 2300 Suncab was introduced by its builders, Draco AS of Norway in 1977. B A Peters & Partners imported about 100 into the UK up to 1984.

Like the smaller Draco 2000, the 2300 is a fast weekender, with a large and comfortable cockpit and a two-berth cabin. The extra length has been used to provide a separate toilet compartment and a fitted galley.

Hull shape is medium-vee. Engine installations vary; always a single outdrive, always Volvo, but ranging from 120 to 200hp in petrol engines and 125 to 150hp in diesels. The standard 145hp petrol engine gives a top speed of about 25 knots. With the popular 200hp petrol option the boat can do over 30 knots.

Length overall	23ft 0in (7.01m)
Beam	8ft 6in (2.59m)
Draught	2ft 9in (0.84m)
Hull/deck material	GRP

FAIREY HUNTRESS

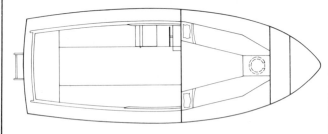

Length overall	23ft 0in (7.01m)
Beam	8ft 6in (2.59m)
Draught	2ft 6in (0.76m)
Hull/deck material	wood

ONE of Fairey Marine's best customers for their Fairey Huntress was the Royal Navy, who ordered them for use as high-speed admirals' barges. But this Hamble River boatyard also built about 100 Huntresses for the pleasure boat market, as express cruisers — the first in 1959, the last in 1970. The hull is based on one of the constant-deadrise deep-vee designs by American Ray Hunt, and is of hot-moulded agba veneer construction. Like its larger sisters, the Huntsmans 29 and 31, the Huntress proved its high-speed seaworthiness through regular appearances in the Cowes-Torquay and other offshore powerboat races during the 1960s.

There are two berths in a small cabin, which has a separate toilet compartment. More than half the boat is taken up by a large cockpit.

The first boats were fitted with either a 120hp Perkins diesel inboard, giving a top speed of about 22 knots, or a 215hp Dearborn Interceptor petrol engine (27 knots). From 1964 the standard engine was the 135hp (later uprated to 145hp) Perkins (20 knots), but some later boats are powered by 175hp Perkins (29 knots).

IP23/24

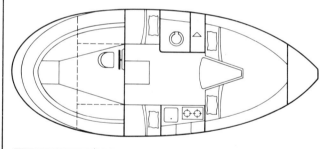

	IP23	IP24
Length overall	23ft 0in (7.01m)	24ft 0in (7.32m)
Beam	9ft 0in (2.74m)	9ft 2in (2.80)
Draught	2ft 7in (0.79m)	2ft 7in (0.79m)
Hull/deck material	GRP	GRP

ISLAND Plastics, of Ryde, Isle of Wight, launched the IP23 in 1970 and the IP24 (virtually identical, but slightly larger) five years later. Both boats were supplied as mouldings for completion by DIY owners or other boatyards. The photographs and drawings are of the 24.

Most of the 2000-plus boats sold to date have been fitted out for fishing, but about 400 have ended up as motor cruisers or motor sailers. Among the boatbuilders who have fitted out the boats as motor cruisers have been Chesford Marine (the **Chesford Fisherman**) and Mike Tilney (the **Tilney 24**). The IP24 moulds are now owned by the Hayling Yacht Co, who supply moulds or completed boats.

The standard cruiser superstructure moulding allows a wheelhouse aft, open to a small cockpit, and room for four berths, a galley and a separate toilet compartment.

Hull form is round-bilge, strictly displacement. A variety of single diesels have been fitted. Hayling Yacht recommend a maximum 30hp, quite sufficient to push the boat up to her hull speed of just over 7 knots.

RELCRAFT 23

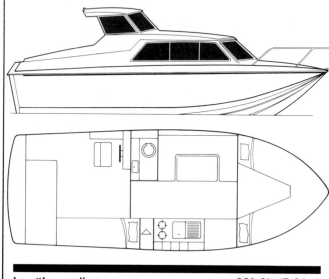

THE Relcraft 23 Sapphire was the first of the extensive range of small fast cruisers designed by John Moxham and built by Reliance Marine. Just under 300 Sapphires were produced between 1970 and 1980. The Relcraft 23 Opal and Relcraft 23 Coral were variations on the same hull, of which Reliance built a total of about 120.

The Sapphire has either four or five berths, the five-berth version having a quarter berth stretching under one of the cockpit seats. The cabin is open-plan but with a separate toilet compartment. The small aft cockpit has a hard top over the helm position. The Opal has a large cockpit and a small two-berth cabin. The Coral comes somewhere between the other two in its size of cabin and cockpit, and has four berths; some Corals were built with a flying bridge. The photograph and drawings show the Sapphire.

The hull is deep-vee with concave chines that act as mini stabilising sponsons. Power comes from a single petrol outdrive, usually Volvo or Mercruiser, of 120 to 220hp. With 200hp the top speed is about 25 knots.

Length overall	23ft 0in (7.01m)
Beam	9ft 6in (2.90m)
Draught	2ft 0in (0.61m)
Hull/deck material	GRP

SHETLAND BLACK PRINCE

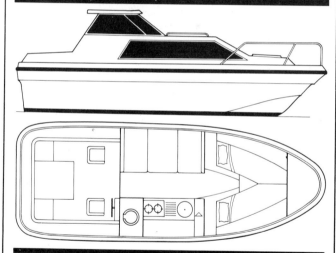

THE Shetland Black Prince was designed by Colin Mudie and built by Shetland Boats, who produced about 200 of this model between 1978 and 1982.

The Black Prince sleeps four — two right forward on vee berths and two on a double berth converted from a dinette — and has a small toilet compartment and a fair-sized galley.

The hull shape — medium-vee with angled down chines — is almost gull-wing in design, with the benefits of improved stability and added lift. A variety of single outdrive engines were installed, including 200hp Volvo and 240hp OMC petrol engines, giving top speeds of nearly 37 knots and over 40 knots respectively, and a 130hp Volvo diesel, which gave over 25 knots during builders' trials.

Length overall	23ft 0in (7.01m)
Beam	8ft 0in (2.44m)
Draught	2ft 9in (0.84m)
Hull/deck material	GRP

SUNSEEKER 235

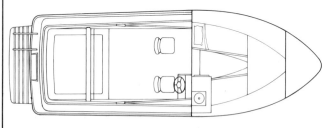

MORE a large sportsboat with occasional overnight accommodation than a real motor cruiser, the Sunseeker 235 is nearly all open cockpit, with a small cabin under the foredeck. Top powerboat designer Don Shead designed the 235 (and all the current range of Sunseekers) and Poole Powerboats (now Sunseeker International) built 117 of them, between 1979 and 1984.

The cockpit seats up to six people and right aft there is a sunlounging area over the engine compartment. The cabin has two vee berths which can be converted into a double — or even a friendly treble — with space for a galley and a toilet under one of the berths.

Hull shape is deep-vee. Power comes from single or twin Volvo petrol outdrive installations, such as 1 × 225hp, giving a top speed of 30 to 31 knots, 1 × 260 (35 knots) or 2 × 145 (34 to 35 knots); or a single Volvo diesel, typically 165hp (28 knots).

Length overall	23ft 0in (7.01m)
Beam	8ft 0in (2.44m)
Draught	1ft 8in (0.51m)
Hull/deck material	GRP

SEAMASTER 23

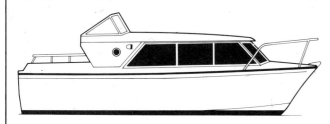

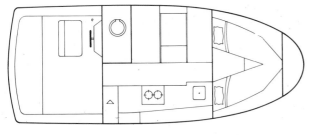

THE Seamaster 23 was introduced in 1968 and was in production until 1975, by which time builders Seamaster Ltd had turned out 345 examples. Popular as a river boat, the 23 is also capable of estuary and coastal cruising in reasonable conditions.

There's accommodation for four in a spacious open-plan cabin. The cockpit is fairly small with a helm seat and a bench seat across the stern.

The hull is of medium-vee configuration with a long shallow keel. Various single outdrive engines were fitted, including a 50hp Perkins diesel or 40 to 55hp Ford or BMC petrol engines, driving the boat at up to about 10 knots. A few are powered by 120 or 130hp Volvo petrol engines, pushing top speed up to about 20 knots.

Length overall	23ft 2in (7.06m)
Beam	9ft 2in (2.80m)
Draught	1ft 6in (0.46m)
Hull/deck material	GRP

FREEMAN 23

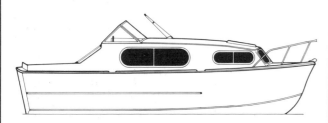

Length overall	23ft 3in (7.09m)
Beam	7ft 6in (2.29m)
Draught	2ft 0in (0.61m)
Hull/deck material	GRP

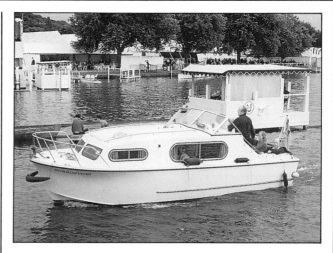

A SUCCESSOR to the Freeman 22, the Freeman 23 was launched in 1970. John Freeman (Marine) built about 700 examples up to 1975. The boat is similar in appearance to the 22 but without the step in the deck line.

The layout is also similar, with four berths in a cabin that is basically open-plan but can be divided into two by opening the hanging locker door out across the boat.

Hull shape is shallow-vee. The 23 is basically a river cruiser but is capable of short esturial or sheltered coastal passages in fair weather. The boat was most commonly fitted with a 35hp Ford Watermota petrol engine or a 50hp Perkins diesel, giving speeds up to 9 or 10 knots.

SENIOR 23

Length overall	23ft 3in (7.09m)
Beam	8ft 6in (2.59m)
Draught	2ft 0in (0.61m)
Hull/deck material	GRP

SENIOR MARINE of Southampton built about 250 Senior 23s between 1966 and 1978, most of them in bare hull and superstructure form for completion by individuals or other yards. Eastwood Marine's **Eastwood 24** and Marina Boats' **Marina 23** were both based on the Senior 23 hull. Seniors/Eastwoods/Marinas were sold for use on rivers, or in estuarial or sheltered coastal waters, in fair weather.

The usual layout has four berths — two vee berths forward and a convertible dinette — and an open helm position in the aft cockpit.

Designed by John Bennett, the hull has shallow-vee underwater sections with a keel to give low-speed directional stability. Various single inboard engines were fitted, petrol or diesel, usually of between 20 and 50hp, giving a top speed of 7-9 knots.

NELSON 23-26

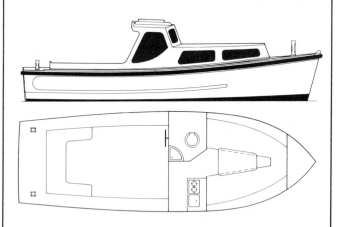

Length overall	23ft 6in (7.16m)
Beam	8ft 3in (2.51m)
Draught	2ft 0in (0.61m)
Hull/deck material	wood

LAUNCHED in 1958, the 23 was the first of the famous Nelson range of motorboats. Their distinctive sheer and well proportioned superstructure is a hallmark of the late Peter Thornycroft and his company, TT Boat Designs, but unlike later Nelsons these were wooden boats. Most were built by Keith, Nelson of Bembridge, Isle of Wight. Altogether between 25 and 30 were built (including some of the same design but up to four feet longer — the photograph shows a 26-footer), the last one in 1966. Construction was in mahogany planking, clinker-laid on American rock elm frames.

The boats have a large aft cockpit, open-backed wheelhouse and cabin with two berths, galley and toilet compartment.

Hull shape is round-bilge. Engines are mostly Perkins or air-cooled Lister diesels, ranging in power from about 20 to 70hp. Top speed with 20hp is about 6½ knots — the boat's maximum displacement speed. With 70hp the boat will start to rise up its bow wave to a top speed of about 9 knots, but will be restricted to 6½ or 7 for comfortable cruising.

FJORD 24 WEEKENDER

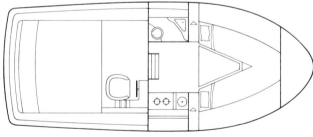

THE Fjord 24 Weekender, designed by Eivind Amble and built by Fjord Plast, both of Norway, was a trailblazer. It was the first production cruiser with a mid-cabin or mini-cabin under the forward, raised part of the cockpit, accessible from the main cabin. Nowadays such an arrangement is to be found on many 20ft to 30ft sports cruisers. Over a hundred 24 Weekenders were imported into the UK, between 1968 and 1980.

The Fjord 24 Weekender sleeps four — two in the main cabin and two in the mid-cabin.

Hull shape is deep-vee and the boat is powered by twin outdrive engines, commonly 130hp petrol Volvos in the earlier boats, 145hp in the later ones, reaching speeds of about 30 and 32 knots respectively. Some have twin 106hp Volvo diesels with which top speed should be 25 to 26 knots.

Length overall	23ft 7in (7.19m)
Beam	9ft 7in (2.92m)
Draught	2ft 9in (08.84m)
Hull/deck material	GRP

HUNTON GAZELLE 23/27

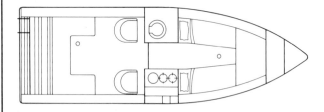

	Gazelle 23	Gazelle 27
Length overall	23ft 7in (7.19m)	27ft 1in (8.25m)
Beam	7ft 8in (2.34m)	7ft 9in (2.36m)
Draught	1ft 9in (0.53m)	2ft 0in (0.61m)
Hull/deck material	GRP	GRP

THE Hunton Gazelle 23 was the first of Hunton Powerboats' Gazelle range of ultra-fast, deep-vee sports cruisers that proved themselves with a string of successes in National Cruiser Class racing. The Gazelle 27 is a stretched version of the 23 and it also had a number of Cruiser Class racing successes. The 23 was introduced in 1978 and the 27 in 1981, a total of 30 being built up to 1984, when they were superseded by a new 28-footer.

At least half the boat's length — more like two-thirds in the case of the 27 — is taken up by cockpit but there is a reasonably roomy cabin with two berths, galley and separate toilet compartment. Two long seats can be used as occasional berths under the cockpit canopy.

Engine installations — all petrol outdrives and mostly Mercruisers — range from 1 × 140hp to 2 × 140hp in the 23, giving top speeds of about 31 knots and nearly 40 knots; and 1 × 230hp to 2 × 260hp in the 27, the latter driving the boat at over 50 knots.

SEAMASTER 725

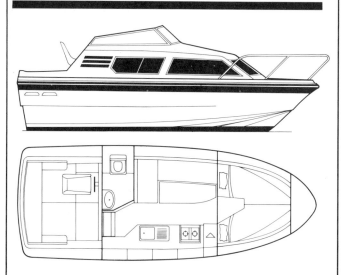

Length overall	23ft 10in (7.26m)
Beam	9ft 1in (2.77m)
Draught	2ft 9in (0.84m)
Hull/deck material	GRP

THE Seamaster 725 was introduced in 1980, just a year before the builders, Seamaster Ltd, ceased trading (later to be revived as a division of Viking Mouldings). However, nearly fifty 725s were built in that short period, and the boat is still available from the new Seamaster Ltd, who have built a further 30 examples.

The boat sleeps four in an open-plan cabin, with a well-equipped galley and a separate toilet compartment. There's seating for three or four, including the driver, in the small aft cockpit.

Hull shape is medium-vee, with a three-quarter-length shallow keel. Single or twin petrol engines or single diesels — all Volvos, all outdrives — were fitted. The most popular installation was a pair of 120hp petrol engines, driving the boat at up to about 25 knots.

ANCAS QUEEN 24

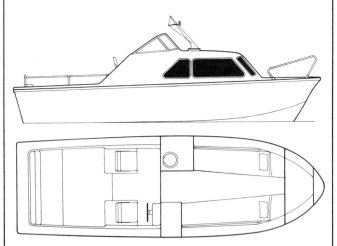

THE Ancas Queen 24 dates from the early 1960s, built in Norway and imported into the UK by Dell Quay and later by Thomas Nelson Yachts. In 1969 the builders, Ancas, were taken over by another Norwegian builder, Selco, and the boat became the Selqueen 24. About 40 Ancas Queen and Selqueen 24s were imported. The boat changed its name again in 1972, when Fjord Plast took over Selco, but few Fjordqueen 24s found their way into the UK.

There is accommodation for two, in quite a spacious cabin with separate toilet compartment; the galley, in true Scandinavian style, being up in the cockpit under one of the seats. The cockpit is also spacious, with seating for five or six, and either the whole area or just the forward end, including the helmsman's and navigator's seat (and the galley), can be covered by a canopy.

The boat has a medium-vee hull with a long, shallow keel. Standard engine is a 130hp Volvo petrol outdrive, which should give a top speed of over 25 knots. Some later boats were powered by a pair of the same engines, driving the boat at up to 30 knots.

Length overall	24ft 0in (7.32m)
Beam	7ft 9in (2.36m)
Draught	2ft 1in (0.63m)
Hull/deck material	GRP

DAUNTLESS 24

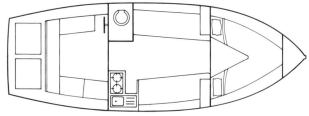

Length overall	24ft 0in (7.32m)
Beam	8ft 6in (2.59m)
Draught	2ft 0in (0.61m)
Hull/deck material	wood

FROM 1948 to 1980 the Dauntless Co of Canvey Island built a range of motor cruisers, fishing boats and sailing boats, all of traditional wooden construction, using mahogany planking clinker laid on ash. The Dauntless 24 was the last and largest of these, launched in 1965. A total of 48 were built.

The boat has four berths in two cabins, with a simple galley and a small toilet compartment. Out in the cockpit there is some shelter from a hard top at the helm position.

The round-bilge hull shape is designed purely for displacement performance, that is with a top speed of no more than 6 knots. Various single inboard engines were fitted, most commonly a 35hp BMC Captain diesel.

DOLPHIN 24

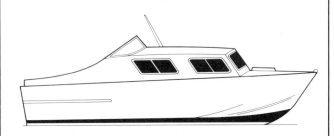

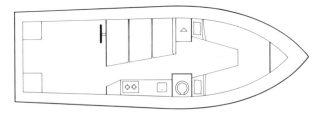

A LARGER version of the Dolphin 20, the Dolphin 24 Wide Beam (the full name distinguishes it from two 24ft canal cruisers from the same range) was introduced by builders Brooklands Aviation in 1968. The boat was only in production for five years, but 200 were built in that time. Construction is of marine ply. There was no MkII, GRP-hulled version, as there was with the 20.

The boat sleeps four, with two berths in a forecabin and a convertible dinette-cum-double berth in the saloon.

Hull shape is shallow- to medium-vee. Power comes from petrol outdrive engines, either single or occasionally twin 80hp Mangoletsi Fords, or a single 90hp OMC. A single Mangoletsi would have given a top speed of 22 to 24 knots with the boat light-loaded, the OMC another knot or two.

Length overall	24ft 0in (7.32m)
Beam	8ft 1in (2.46m)
Draught	1ft 6in (0.46m)
Hull/deck material	wood

CORONET 24

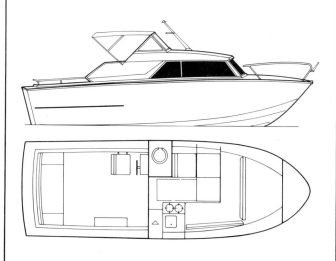

A FAST cruiser with a racing pedigree, the Coronet 24 Cabin was based on a Jim Wynne and Walt Walters deep-vee hull design. One of these boats took part in four Cowes-Torquay powerboat races, once finishing 10th overall, and in the 1969 Round Britain powerboat race Coronet 24s finished 8th and 9th overall. The 24 Cabin was one of a large range of motor cruisers (including two other 24-footers, the 24 Family Cruiser, which had more accommodation, and the 24 Midi, which had less) built by Botved Boats in Denmark. About 500 were imported into the UK from 1964 to 1973, initially by Dell Quay Sales and then by Poole Powerboats (now Sunseeker International).

The standard boat has an open-cockpit helm position, though a hardtop was available as an option. In the open-plan cabin there are four berths and a galley, with a separate toilet compartment.

Engines are twin Volvo petrol outdrives, most commonly 2 × 110hp on the earlier boats, 2 × 130hp on the later ones, giving top speeds of about 28 and 30 knots respectively.

Length overall	24ft 2in (7.37m)
Beam	8ft 0in (2.44m)
Draught	2ft 3in (0.69m)
Hull/deck material	GRP

FREEMAN 24/750

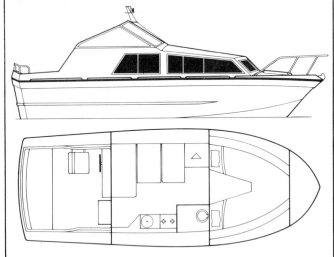

THE Freeman 24 superseded the Freeman 23. The boat has a very different hull, of medium-vee configuration and considerably beamier than the 23's. The superstructure is different too, its rakish lines in complete contrast to the soft curves of the 23. And you can drive the boat from the shelter of an open-backed wheelhouse. John Freeman (Marine) built over 1000 Freeman 24s, from 1975 to 1984. From about 1980 they preferred to call the boat the Freeman 750. The boat is primarily a river cruiser but is capable of making esturial and sheltered coastal passages in fair weather.

The interior layout is similar to the 23's, with four berths in an open-plan cabin in which the forward berths can be isolated by opening the hanging locker door across the boat.

Most 24s are powered by single inboard engines, petrol Ford Watermotas from 30 to 63hp, or 55hp Perkins diesels, giving speeds of 9 to 10 knots. Two of the same push speeds up to 12 to 14 knots.

Length overall	24ft 6in (7.47m)
Beam	9ft 0in (2.74m)
Draught	2ft 0in (0.61m)
Hull/deck material	GRP

PRINCESS 25

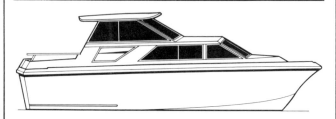

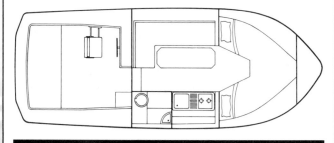

DESIGNED by John Bennett, the Princess 25 was a successor to the Pilgrim 25. Marine Projects built nearly 250 Princess 25s between 1974 and 1981.

There is accommodation for four in an interior layout which is basically open-plan but has a full-width folding partition with which the two forward vee berths can be isolated. The open-backed wheelhouse and stern cockpit are on the same level. Some boats have a large roll-up sunroof in the wheelhouse top.

The hull is deep-vee at midships and medium-vee aft. A range of single petrol outdrive engines was offered. Top speed with a 130hp Volvo should be about 16 knots. A few boats were fitted with twin 130s, giving speeds of more than 25 knots.

Length overall	24ft 8in (7.52m)
Beam	9ft 2in (2.80m)
Draught	1ft 6in (0.46m)
Hull/deck material	GRP

SEAMASTER CADET

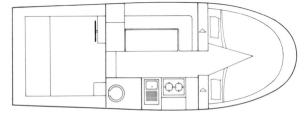

TWO more, nearly identical, boats in Seamaster's extensive range, the Seamaster Cadet and **Seamaster Admiral** were launched in 1961 and 1963 respectively. About 400 were built, of both models, up to 1967.

The Cadet has an open-plan cabin with four berths — two forward and a convertible dinette-cum-double. The Admiral, which was originally called the Cadet MkII, has a similar arrangement but the two forward berths are separated by bulkheads and a door into their own cabin.

Hull shape is shallow-vee with a long shallow keel. The boats were fitted with single or twin petrol engines of 40 to 65hp, or a single 40hp BMC diesel. With a single engine top speed is 8 or 9 knots, with twins 10 to 12 knots.

The photograph and drawings show the Cadet.

Length overall	24ft 8in (7.52m)
Beam	9ft 2in (2.80m)
Draught	1ft 10in (0.56m)
Hull/deck material	GRP

FAIRLINE FURY

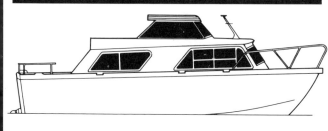

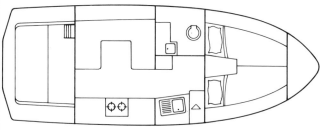

Length overall	24ft 9in (7.54m)
Beam	8ft 9in (2.67m)
Draught	2ft 2in (0.66m)
Hull/deck material	GRP

THE original Fairline Fury (as distinct from the Fairline Fury 26 and Sunfury 26) was a radical boat when launched in 1968. Designed by John Bennett, the Fury had its single helm position up on a kind of flying bridge (usually under a small shelter), not over the wheelhouse in the conventional manner but at midships, recessed into the superstructure. Oundle Marina, the boatbuilding side of which became Fairline Boats in 1971, built 139 Furys, up to 1974.

With its unusual helm position and longer than usual superstructure, the Fury has more interior space than one would expect to see on a boat of its size. There are four berths, two in a forward cabin and two, in the form of a dinette-cum-double, in the saloon. There is also a comparatively roomy toilet compartment and a galley with a generous amount of storage space and work surface.

Furys have a modified medium-vee hull with rounded sections aft and broad chine flats, and are most commonly powered by Volvo petrol outdrives from 1 x 105hp to 2 x 115hp, the latter giving a top speed of 25-26 knots.

SUNSEEKER 25

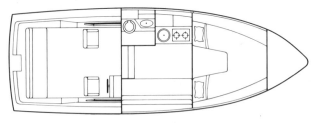

Length overall	24ft 9in (7.54m)
Beam	8ft 5in (2.57m)
Draught	2ft 0in (0.61m)
Hull/deck material	GRP

POOLE Powerboats (later Sunseeker International) introduced the Sunseeker 25 Offshore, a fast sports cruiser, in 1980, and built 50 of them up to 1986.

The boat has four berths, with two vee berths forward and a settee which can be pulled out into a double. Out in the spacious cockpit there's seating for five or six, including the driver.

Don Shead designed the 25 for high-speed performance, with a deep-vee hull. Among a variety of outdrive installations the most common are: a pair of 175hp Volvo petrol engines, driving the boat at up to 32-33 knots; a single 260hp petrol Volvo, producing about the same performance; and a single 165hp Volvo diesel (28 knots).

A dayboat-cum-weekender version of the boat, called the Sunseeker 25 Portofino, has a larger cockpit and smaller cabin.

ALBIN 25

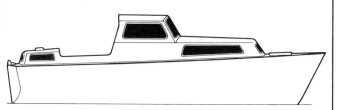

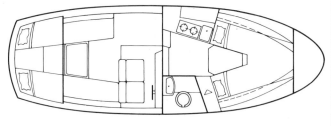

ALBIN Marine of Sweden built over 2000 Albin 25s between 1968 and 1978, of which about 100 were imported into the UK. Many individuals brought in bare mouldings for home completion, attracted by the workmanlike lines of this double-ended displacement cruiser.

The boat sleeps four. There are two berths in the main cabin, which has a galley and a separate toilet compartment, and two in a small cabin aft of the centre cockpit and open-backed wheelhouse.

Early boats were fitted with a single 20hp Albin diesel inboard, which gave a top speed of 8½ knots. Later the standard engine became a 36hp Volvo diesel, which increased top speed to about 10 knots.

Length overall	25ft 0in (7.62m)
Beam	8ft 6in (2.59m)
Draught	2ft 4in (0.71m)
Hull/deck material	GRP

BERTRAM 25

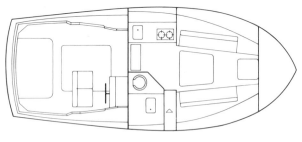

Length overall	25ft 0in (7.62m)
Beam	9ft 11in (3.02m)
Draught	2ft 5in (0.74m)
Hull/deck material	GRP

IN the first Cowes-Torquay Powerboat Race, in 1961, a standard Bertram 25 cruiser, *Yo-Yo*, finished second to a standard Christina 25. Both boats were of the then revolutionary full-length deep-vee hull design created by American naval architect Ray Hunt. The Bertrams were built by the Bertram Yacht Company in Florida. Their UK agents, Thomas Nelson Yacht Agency, imported about forty 25s between 1961 and 1966 (Bertram's are still building fast motorboats but few have been imported in recent years).

The Express Cruiser version, which accounted for nearly all the Bertram 25s imported into the UK, has an open helm position in a large aft cockpit. The cabin sleeps up to four — two settee berths, the backs of which lift up to form two upper bunk berths — and a separate toilet compartment.

Power comes from twin outdrive petrol engines, commonly Volvos or Mercruisers, from 110hp to 150hp each, giving top speeds of about 30 to 35 knots.

BIRCHWOOD INTERCEPTER /25

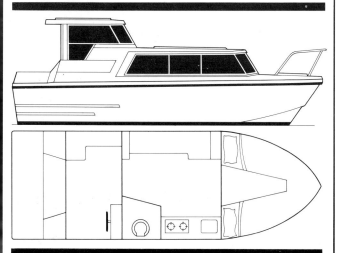

Length overall	25ft 0in (7.62m)
Beam	9ft 3in (2.82m)
Draught	2ft 0in (0.61m)
Hull/deck material	GRP

WHEN it was launched in 1968, the Birchwood Intercepter was the largest of Birchwood Boat Co's range (now, as Birchwood Boat International, the company builds craft up to 54ft). In 1975 the boat was modified and renamed Birchwood 25. About 1500 Intercepters and 25s were built, up to 1980.

An open-plan cabin has berths for four, while a settee can be pulled out into a double, warm-weather berth, under the cockpit canopy. Most Intercepters have a hard-top helm shelter, while the 25s have a more extensive shelter which amounts to an open-backed wheelhouse.

Hull shape is shallow-vee. Most boats were fitted with a single outdrive, usually a 115 or 130hp petrol Volvo in the Intercepter (the latter giving a top speed of 18 to 20 knots), and one of several options up to twin 225hp OMCs (which should give up to 26 to 28 knots) in the 25. Twin outdrive options were also offered in the 25, up to 2 × 145hp (28 to 30 knots) and some 25s were fitted with an 80hp Ford inboard petrol engine (10 knots).

CHRISTINA 25

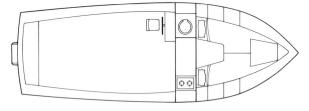

Length overall	25ft 0in (7.62m)
Beam	9ft 4in (2.84m)
Draught	2ft 7in (0.79m)
Hull/deck material	wood

WHEN Tommy Sopwith won the first Cowes-Torquay Powerboat Race in 1961 he did it in a Christina 25. Christinas were built by Bruce Campbell Ltd, of Hamble, the first in 1958 and the last (of about 70) in 1963, when the company went into liquidation. The boat was based on the Fairey Huntress deep-vee hull, designed by American Ray Hunt. For the first two years the hulls were supplied by Fairey and were of hot-moulded construction. Then they were produced, cold-moulded, by Walter Lawrence, and later still were moulded in GRP by Halmatic. When Bruce Campbell went into liquidation Halmatic launched their own GRP version, called the **Ocean 25**, of which they built a dozen.

Most of the Christina is taken up with a very large cockpit and there is accommodation for just two in a basic cabin. The Ocean 25 has a rather larger cabin, with four berths.

Christinas were built with a wide variety of inboard engines — single and twin, petrol and diesel — from 1 x 170hp to 2 x 325hp, the latter giving over 40 knots. Ocean 25s were commonly fitted with twin 120hp Volvo petrol outdrives.

DRACO 2500

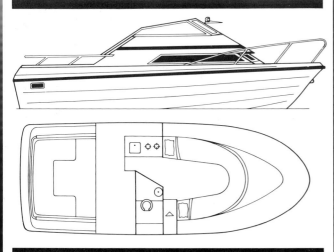

Length overall	25ft 0in (7.62m)
Beam	9ft 2in (2.80m)
Draught	2ft 8in (0.81m)
Hull/deck material	GRP

LAUNCHED in 1976 by its Norwegian builders, Draco AS, the Draco 2500 Twincab was imported into the UK firstly by Northshore Yacht Yards and then from 1978 by B A Peters & Partners. About 100 were imported up to 1984.

There are four berths in two separate cabins, one of them stretching under the raised helm position in the large cockpit.

The hull is simulated-clinker and the bottom is medium-vee. Engine installations vary widely (though are all outdrives) — single or twin, petrol or diesel, Volvo or Mercruiser, from 1 × 130hp to 2 × 175hp. Two 145hp Volvo petrol engines give a top speed of over 30 knots.

The current Draco range includes a 2500 but it has a completely different hull, superstructure and layout.

PILGRIM 25

Length overall	25ft 0in (7.62m)
Beam	9ft 2in (2.80m)
Draught	1ft 6in (0.46m)
Hull/deck material	GRP

MARINE Projects of Plymouth built over 200 Pilgrim 25s between 1970 and 1974, when the boat was superseded by the Princess 25.

There are four berths in an open-plan layout (a full-width folding partition can be pulled across to isolate the two forward berths), with a largish stern cockpit and open-backed wheelhouse on one level. On some boats most of the wheelhouse top takes the form of a large roll-up sunroof; an optional alternative to the standard hard top.

Hull shape is medium-vee and the boats were fitted variously with single and twin, petrol and diesel outdrive engines. The most common installation is a pair of 120hp Volvo petrol engines, giving over 20 knots. With a single 50hp Perkins diesel the boat would do 11 to 12 knots.

TRIANA 25

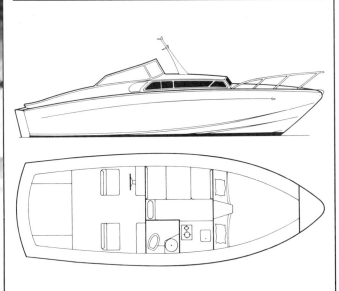

THE Triana 25 was designed by Renato 'Sonny' Levi, the successful powerboat designer. From 1963 to 1968 the hulls were moulded by Tylers and fitted out by Trident Marine, who turned out 25 boats. The moulds were then taken over by a new firm, Triana Boats, who renamed the boat Triana Tropica, and this is still in (limited) production today. Another 80 or so have been built to date. Though not intended for racing, Trianas did have some competitive successes, including a 15th overall (*Miss Bovril II*) in the 1969 Round Britain race.

Trianas have been built with two different accommodation layouts, one with four berths and the other (including most of the later boats) with just two, in rather more comfort.

The hull is unmistakably a Levi design, with very deep-vee underwater sections, sharply raked stem and reverse sheer. Most of the early boats were fitted with two 120hp petrol Volvo outdrives, giving a top speed of about 28 knots. Standard engines on the Tropicas are 170hp Volvos, driving the boat at 35 to 40 knots.

Length overall	25ft 0in (7.62m)
Beam	8ft 11in (2.72m)
Draught	2ft 8in (0.81m)
Hull/deck material	GRP

GULF-STREAMER 25

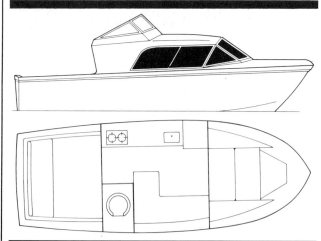

Length overall	25ft 4in (7.72m)
Beam	9ft 0in (2.74m)
Draught	1ft 3in (0.38m)
Hull/deck material	GRP

WHEN the Gulfstreamer 25 was introduced in 1969 it was quite a revolutionary boat. It was one of the first to make extensive use of interior mouldings and it was — and still is — highly unusual for a 25-footer to sport a flying bridge. The boat was designed by John Bennett and built first by Reedcraft and then a number of other companies. About 40 were built altogether, up to 1985.

The cabin is open-plan but with a separate toilet compartment. There is accommodation for four, on a double berth forward (with a removable backrest across it to turn it into a settee) and on two over-and-under bunk berths formed by raising the back of another settee. The flying bridge — which is the only helm position — has seating for two, including the driver, who sits with one leg on each side of the steering and control column.

The hull has a medium-vee bottom. Power comes from single or twin, diesel or petrol outdrives. The most popular installations were single 130hp or twin 115hp Volvo petrol engines, giving top speeds of 22 to 23 and about 30 knots respectively.

NIMBUS 26/2000

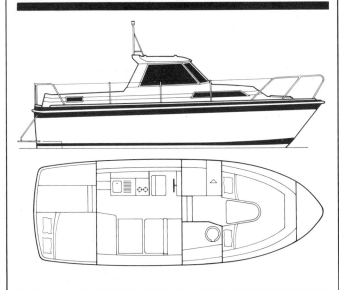

Length overall	25ft 9in (7.85m)
Beam	9ft 4in (2.8m)
Draught	2ft 8in (0.81m)
Hull/deck material	GRP

THE Nimbus 26 was introduced by its Swedish builders, Hansson & Lundbom (now Nimbus Boats) in 1969. It was succeeded in 1982 by the Nimbus 2600, with new hull and deck mouldings and modified interior. About 1700 of the 26s and 2600s have been built to date (the latter is still in production), and about 120 have been imported into the UK by various companies, including current UK Nimbus agents Offshore Powerboats.

Typically Scandinavian in layout, the Nimbus has a galley in the midships cockpit, which runs into an open-backed wheelhouse with large sunroof, the whole area being enclosable with a canopy. The 26 has four berths — two in the forward cabin and two in the aft cabin. The 2600 has an extra berth in the forward cabin, a quarter berth stretching under the wheelhouse.

The boat has a hull that is medium-vee back to midships, very shallow-vee aft, with a short, shallow keel and a skeg. Power comes from a single inboard engine, usually a Volvo diesel: in the 26s 75hp (12 to 13 knots), in the 2600s 105hp (20 knots) or, latterly, 125hp (22 knots).

FREEMAN 26

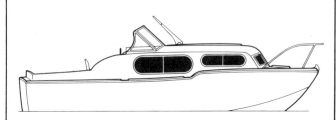

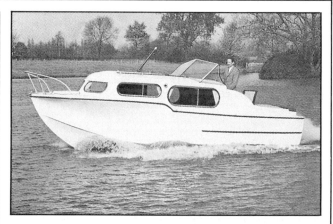

Length overall	25ft 10in (7.87m)
Beam	8ft 10in (2.69m)
Draught	2ft 6in (0.76m)
Hull/deck material	GRP

THE Freeman 26 is one of the older-style Freemans, with rounded superstructure lines and, as on the post-1964 models of the Freeman 22, a step in the deck line. John Freeman (Marine), who had a reputation for high-quality moulding and interior finish, built over 300 between 1965 and 1973. The **Freeman 28**, of which 60 were built, was a development of the 26.

The boat has four berths in an open-plan layout with an open helm position in the aft cockpit.

Hull shape is shallow-vee with a long, shallow keel. Freeman 26s can be found mostly on rivers though they are capable of making passages in estuarial and sheltered coastal waters in fair weather. A single petrol (usually a 50hp Ford Watermota) or diesel (50hp Perkins) drives the boat at up to 10 or 11 knots.

CHRIS-CRAFT 26

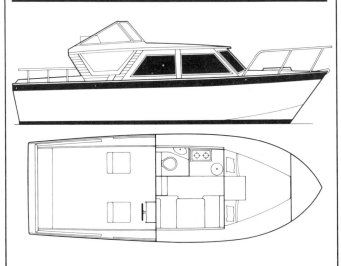

THE Chris-Craft Corporation of America (later called Chris-Craft Industries and now just Chris-Craft following a financial collapse and change of ownership in the late 1970s) are the oldest motor boatbuilding company in the world. They launched their first motorboat in 1874. Their motor cruisers have never been imported into the UK in vast numbers, but during the mid- and late-1960s Carl Ziegler Yacht Agency did bring in several, including about 30 Chris-Craft 26s, which were actually built at the company's factory in Fiumicino, Italy.

There is accommodation for four in what was — and still is — a conventional layout of two vee berths forward and a convertible dinette, all in an open-plan cabin. The helm position is out in the open, in the large aft cockpit.

The boat has a medium-vee hull and is most commonly powered by a single 185hp Chris-Craft marinised GM diesel, which gives a top speed of 26 to 30 knots.

Length overall	26ft 0in (7.92m)
Beam	9ft 4in (2.84m)
Draught	1ft 10in (0.56m)
Hull/deck material	GRP

FLETCHER ZINGARO 26

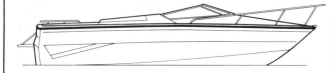

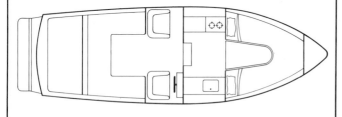

THE Fletcher Zingaro 26 was built in three different versions: Sedan, Flybridge and Express. By some way the most popular of the three was the one with the least accommodation, the Express (illustrated), a two-berth high-performance sports cruiser. Fletcher International launched the Zingaro 26 at the 1976 London Boat Show and built 80 boats up to 1982.

Sedan and Flybridge Zingaros have four permanent berths — and a couple of occasional ones — with outside helm positions, up on a flying bridge in the case of the Flybridge version. The Express has just two berths in a very basic cabin, with a toilet under one of the bunks and space for a small galley, but it does have a vast cockpit, in which up to 10 people can sit, or two can sleep under an overall canopy.

Hull shape is deep- to medium-vee (deep from forward to midships, medium aft). The Zingaro — the Express at least — had a reputation as one of the best fast seagoing boats of its type. Various engines have been fitted, all outdrives and mostly petrol, ranging from 1×230hp to 2×260hp, the latter driving the boat at up to 50 knots.

Length overall	26ft 0in (7.92m)
Beam	9ft 1in (2.77m)
Draught	2ft 9in (0.84m)
Hull/deck material	GRP

KINGSWIFT 26

BETWEEN 1969 and 1975 William Osborne of Littlehampton, the RNLI lifeboat builders, produced 36 Kingswift 26 motor cruisers, of which 16 were supplied as bare hulls with deck and superstructure kits for home completion. Hulls are GRP, deck and superstructure are marine ply on mahogany frames. A MkII version, of which only two were built, is all GRP.

The Kingswift sleeps four, with two berths in a small forward cabin and two in the saloon, in the form of a convertible dinette or a pull-out settee. There is a large aft cockpit, which unusually gives direct access to the toilet compartment. The helm area is covered with a wheelshelter.

Hull shape is medium-vee. Power comes from twin outdrive engines, most commonly 50hp Perkins diesels, which should give a top speed of 15 to 16 knots. A couple of boats were fitted with twin 130hp BMW petrol engines, giving a top speed of 23 to 25 knots.

Length overall	26ft 0in (7.92m)
Beam	9ft 10in (3.00m)
Draught	2ft 0in (0.61m)
Hull/deck material	GRP/wood or GRP

RELCRAFT 26 AMETHYST

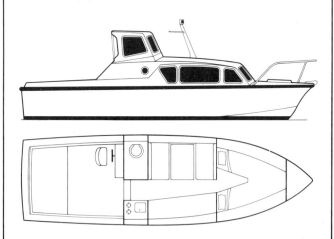

DESIGNED by John Moxham, as were all the boats in the Relcraft range from Reliance Marine, the Relcraft 26 Amethyst is a stretched version of the 23 Sapphire and was launched in 1980. About 70 were built over a three-year period.

The boat sleeps four in an open-plan cabin. Much of the boat is taken up with a vast aft cockpit, with a hard top over the forward end to shelter the helmsman.

Hull shape is deep-vee with concave chines that act like sponsons to give added lift and stability. Engine installations vary, though they are all outdrives. Single or twin, petrol or diesel engines have been fitted, from 1 × 120hp to 2 × 140hp, the latter giving a top speed of over 25 knots.

Length overall	26ft 0in (7.92m)
Beam	9ft 6in (2.90m)
Draught	2ft 4in (0.71m)
Hull/deck material	GRP

HARDY 25

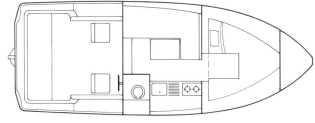

A LARGER but younger sister to the Hardy Family Pilot, the Hardy 25 was introduced in 1982, since when Hardy Marine have built over 100.

An open-plan cabin has four berths, including two vee berths convertible to a double forward and a double berth formed by converting the dinette. There's an open-backed wheelhouse and largish aft cockpit, and as on the Family Pilot the raised topsides form an effective bulwark around the sidedecks.

Colin Mudie designed the boat, giving her rounded sections forward but shallow vee, planing sections from midships aft, and a long, shallow keel for directional stability at low speeds. Most Hardy 25s are powered by single outdrives, typically a 120hp Volvo petrol engine which drives the boat at up to about 23 knots. An outboard version has a well that will take a single outboard of up to 100hp or two up to 60hp. Twin 50hp outboards would give a top speed of about 22 knots.

Length overall	26ft 3in (8.00m)
Beam	9ft 0in (2.74m)
Draught	2ft 5in (0.74m)
Hull/deck material	GRP

SENIOR 26

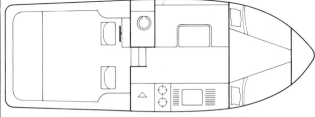

Length overall	26ft 3in (8.00m)
Beam	8ft 6in (2.59m)
Draught	2ft 3in (0.69m)
Hull/deck material	GRP

SENIOR Marine built about 250 Senior 26s, between 1963 and 1978. Most were both moulded and fitted out by the manufacturers, but some were supplied as bare mouldings for completion by do-it-yourself owners or other builders, including RLM Marine of Chertsey. Their Senior-based **RLM 27 Seychelles** remained in production until 1982, the mouldings produced by Midland Mouldings in latter years.

There are berths for four, either in an open-plan layout, as in the Senior Marine version, or with a separate two-berth forecabin, as in the RLM Seychelles. The standard Senior boat has a small open-backed wheelhouse, the Seychelles an open helm position.

Common on rivers and in tidal waters, the boats were fitted with a single inboard diesel — ideal for river cruising — or with single or twin outdrives. For an owner wanting to use the boat in coastal waters, two 50hp outdrive diesels should give a top speed of between 13 and 15 knots.

FAIRLINE FURY 26

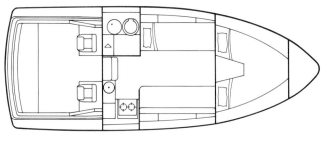

THE first of many Fairlines to be designed by Bernard Olesinski, the Fairline Fury 26 was launched in 1978 and was in production until 1982, when it was replaced by the Sun Fury 26. Fairline Boats built 114 Fury 26s.

The interior resembles a traditional yacht layout with single berths either side of the saloon rather than the ubiquitous convertible dinette (the drop-leaf table between the berths is just a drop-leaf table). There are two more berths in the forward cabin and the cockpit has seating for five or six, including the driver. The deck layout has the unusual feature of inboard, pilot-boat type grabrails in lieu of guardrails.

Typically Olesinski, the hull has deep-vee underwater sections from bow to midships, turning into a medium-vee at the transom, with broad chine flats. A variety of single and twin, petrol and diesel outdrive engines were fitted, most commonly a pair of 140hp petrol Volvos, driving the boat at up to 30 knots.

Length overall	26ft 4in (8.03m)
Beam	10ft 0in (3.05m)
Draught	1ft 11in (0.58m)
Hull/deck material	GRP

FAIRLINE SUNFURY 26

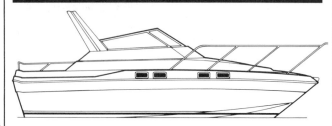

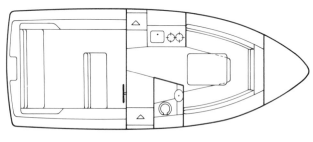

BASED on the same hull as the Fury 26, which it superseded, the Fairline Sun Fury 26 was launched in 1981 and was in production until 1989, during which time Fairline Boats built just under 500.

As in the Fury 26 there are four berths, but in a very different arrangement, with a saloon stretching right forward whose seating area converts into a large double berth, and a mid-cabin with a double berth under the raised forward part of the cockpit. The cockpit itself is larger than on the Fury. The triple helm seat can be reversed to form part of an open-air dinette, and the long seat across the stern can be converted into a sunbed or a fair-weather double berth.

The most popular of many single and twin, petrol and diesel engine options — all Volvo outdrives — have been pairs of 140hp and, later, 150hp petrol engines, giving top speeds of between 28 and 32 knots.

Length overall	26ft 4in (8.03m)
Beam	10ft 0in (3.05m)
Draught	2ft 0in (0.61m)
Hull/deck material	GRP

AQUA-STAR 27

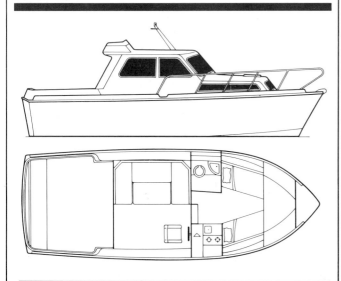

AQUA-STAR Ltd of Guernsey built 300 Aqua-Star 27s from 1970 to 1985, about 200 as motor cruisers, the rest as fishing boats and workboats.

Various motor cruiser versions were built. The Fast Fisherman 27 has a large aft cockpit, open-backed wheelhouse and either two or four berths (two sets of over-and-under bunks), and is aimed at the owner who wants a boat for sea angling as much as for cruising. The Pacesetter 27 has an enclosed wheelhouse-cum-deck saloon and accommodation for two or four plus a possible two more in the wheelhouse/saloon. Mk2 versions of the Pacesetter, introduced in 1982, have a larger wheelhouse/saloon. Another variation is the Luxury Cruiser 27, which has an aft cabin, open-backed midships wheelhouse and four or six berths. The photograph shows a Pacesetter Mk1, the drawings a Pacesetter Mk2.

Hull shape is semi-displacement, round-bilge. Various single diesel/inboard engines were fitted, including a 120hp Ford (giving a top speed of about 12 knots) and a 140hp Volvo (14 to 15 knots).

Length overall	26ft 6in (8.07m)
Beam	9ft 6in (2.90m)
Draught	2ft 10in (0.86m)
Hull/deck material	GRP

COLVIC 26

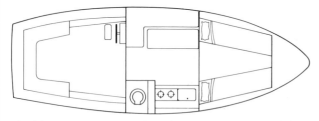

Length overall	26ft 6in (8.08m)
Beam	8ft 8in (2.64m)
Draught	2ft 6in (0.76m)
Hull/deck material	GRP

BETWEEN 1967 and 1985 Colvic Craft, or Ardleigh Laminated Plastics as they used to be known, supplied well over 1000 mouldings of their Colvic 26′ 6″ motor cruiser for boatyards and DIY owners to fit out. Of the yards that used the hulls, the most prolific was West Stockwith Yacht Services. Their version was called the **Northerner Sea Lion** and earned a reputation as a good sea boat.

The usual layout has an aft cockpit, open-backed wheelhouse and accommodation for four.

The round-bilge hull is strictly for displacement performance, the single inboard engines that are fitted — from 25hp up to about 60hp — driving the boat up to a top speed of 7 to 8 knots. Standard engine in the Northerner Sea Lion was a 50hp Perkins diesel.

SEAMASTER 27

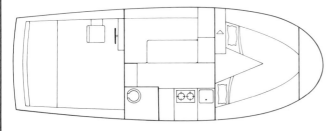

Length overall	26ft 8in (8.13m)
Beam	9ft 4in (2.84m)
Draught	2ft 1in (0.63m)
Hull/deck material	GRP

THE Seamaster 27 was the most popular of all the many motor cruisers that Seamaster Ltd produced. Between 1965 and 1974 they built 600 of the 27s, most of them for use on rivers, although the boat is quite capable of making estuarial and coastal passages in reasonable conditions. Some of the boats were built by Seamaster as bare hulls and superstructures, to be fitted out by other yards, most notably Springfield's of Maidenhead, whose version of the boat was called the **Springfield 27.**

There are four berths — two in a forward cabin and a convertible dinette-cum-double berth in the saloon. The helm position is in the open, in the aft cockpit.

Hull shape is medium- to shallow-vee, with a three-quarter-length shallow keel. Early boats were generally fitted with single (or occasionally twin) Ford or BMC petrol inboards of 40 to 55hp, later ones with a 40hp BMC or 50hp Perkins diesel, giving a top speed of about 10 knots.

SEAMASTER 813

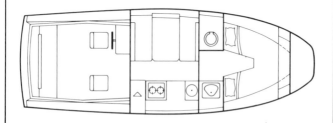

Length overall	26ft 8in (8.13m)
Beam	9ft 1in (2.77m)
Draught	2ft 3in (0.69m)
Hull/deck material	GRP

IN production from 1972 until its builders, Seamaster Ltd, ceased trading in 1981 (later to be revived as a division of Viking Mouldings, at the same location in Great Dunmow, Essex), the Seamaster 813 was most popular as a river cruiser, but it can also venture onto estuarial and coastal waters in fair weather. Nearly 400 were built in that period, and the boat is still available from Viking.

The boat has a large cockpit and open helm position, and down below there are four berths — two in a forward cabin plus a double-cum-dinette in the saloon.

The medium-vee to shallow-vee hull has a long, shallow keel. Some boats were fitted with a single 130hp Volvo petrol outdrive, giving speeds of over 17 knots, but most have more modest inboard engines (diesel or petrol), which are far better for handling at river cruising speeds.

ELYSIAN 27

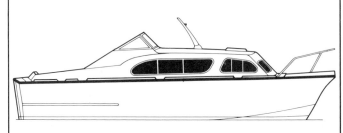

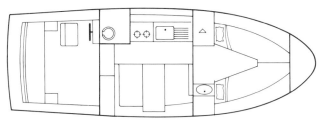

APPLEYARD, Lincoln & Co built the first of over 1600 Elysian 27s in 1963. When they ceased production in the early 1970s the boat was resurrected by J G Meakes, who called it the **Madeira 27**. Bounty Boats took over the moulds in 1975, and have built another 200 or more of what they call the **New Elysian 27** or **Bounty 27**, many fitted out from hulls and kits supplied by them. The photograph shows a Madeira.

There are two main versions, one with a centre cockpit and aft cabin and the other with an aft cockpit and either an open-plan interior layout or saloon and separate forecabin. All versions have four berths. Bounty Boats have only built the boat in aft-cockpit form, some with a hardtop. In 1981 they produced an entirely new deck and superstructure moulding.

With its shallow-vee bottom and long keel, the Elysian is at its best as a displacement boat and is most at home on inland waters, but it is capable of short coastal hops in good weather. Most boats are powered by a single diesel of between 35 and 50hp, commonly a Perkins, giving a top speed of 8 to 9 knots.

Length overall	26ft 10in (8.18m)
Beam	9ft 7in (2.92m)
Draught	2ft 2in (0.66m)
Hull/deck material	GRP

SEAMASTER 820

THE Seamaster 820 was launched in 1979 and was only in production until 1981, when its builders, Seamaster Ltd, ceased trading. Nearly a hundred were built in that time. The boat is now in limited production again, built by a revived Seamaster Ltd, operating as a division of Viking Mouldings.

An open-plan cabin has accommodation for four and the boat is driven from inside an open-backed wheelhouse.

Hull shape is shallow-vee with a three-quarter-length keel. Power comes from single or twin Thornycroft or Perkins diesel inboards of about 50hp, or a single 150hp Volvo petrol outdrive. Top speed with a single diesel should be about 7 knots, with twin diesels 10 to 11 knots, and with the Volvo between 15 and 18 knots.

Length overall	26ft 10in (8.18m)
Beam	10ft 2in (3.10m)
Draught	2ft 4in (0.71m)
Hull/deck material	GRP

BIRCHWOOD 27 COUNTESS

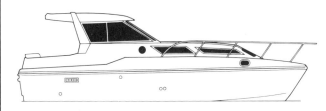

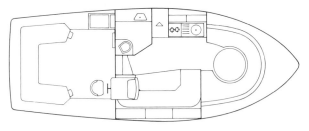

Length overall	27ft 0in (8.23m)
Beam	10ft 2in (3.10m)
Draught	2ft 9in (0.84m)
Hull/deck material	GRP

THE Birchwood Boat Co built around 100 Birchwood 27 Countesses between 1980 and 1984. The boat was designed for both river and coastal cruising.

In the open-plan cabin there are two seating areas which both convert to double berths, and the settee in the aft cockpit can be pulled out into a fair-weather double berth, sheltered by the cockpit canopy. The photograph shows an open-cockpit version of the boat but many were fitted with an optional hard top over the helm position.

Hull shape is basically medium-vee, but with rounded forward sections and a keel to give directional stability at low (river) speeds. Birchwood offered a wide range of engine installations: single or twin, inboard or outdrive, petrol or diesel. Most were fitted with twin diesel outdrives, or twin 140hp petrol Volvos giving a top speed of 28 to 30 knots.

DELL QUAY RANGER

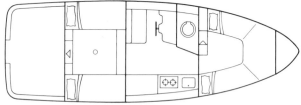

Length overall	27ft 0in (8.23m)
Beam	9ft 0in (2.74m)
Draught	2ft 4in (0.71m)
Hull/deck material	wood

BASED on a hull designed by Ray Hunt (the American designer who introduced the deep-vee hull) and built of hot-moulded mahogany by Fairey Marine, builders of their own range of hot-moulded motor boats (including the famous Fairey Huntsman), the Dell Quay Ranger is a classic mid-1960s fast cruiser. Dell Quay Sales of Itchenor fitted out and sold 140 examples between 1963 and 1968.

The accommodation is split into two two-berth cabins, one either side of the open centre cockpit, which can be enclosed by a canopy. There's a galley in the cockpit, Scandinavian-style, and you enter the single toilet compartment from the cockpit — an unusual but sensible arrangement.

Dell Quay Sales fitted a range of Volvo petrol outdrive engines, from 2 × 110hp to 2 × 180hp, top speeds ranging from just under 25 knots to over 30. A few boats have been re-engined with diesels.

FREEMAN 27

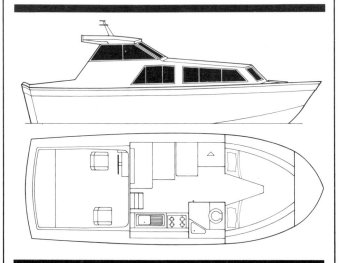

Length overall	27ft 0in (8.23m)
Beam	10ft 1in (3.07m)
Draught	2ft 6in (0.76m)
Hull/deck material	GRP

LAUNCHED in 1978, the Freeman 27 was one of the first boats from John Freeman (Marine) not to have the familiar rounded lines of the earlier models from this once highly successful builder. The 27 has an altogether sportier, more angular look, though the boat's main market was as a river cruiser, albeit one quite capable of cruising, in good weather, down into the estuary and along the coast. Over 300 Freeman 27s were built, the last one in 1984.

Driver and crew can take cover under a wheelshelter, and the open-plan interior layout has four berths, in the common arrangement of convertible dinette and two vee berths forward. John Freeman Marine were known for the excellence of their interior joinery.

Hull shape is medium-vee. Engine options ranged from a single 47hp Ford Watermota petrol inboard, quite sufficient for river cruising, to twin 75hp Volvo diesels, giving a top speed of 15 knots. A long, shallow keel gives good directional stability, a useful feature for river cruising.

PYTHON 27

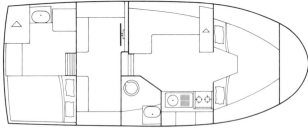

TOUGH Bros of Teddington built 20 Python 27 fast cruisers between 1970 and 1977. The Python is a smaller sister of the Cobra 33.

There are three versions: one designed primarily as a sports fisherman with large cockpit and just two berths forward; another with four berths in an open-plan cabin; and another with six berths, including two in an aft cabin. Most of the boats — in all versions — have an open-backed wheelhouse. The photograph and drawings are of the aft-cabin version.

The hull is deep-vee with a marked flare in the bows. Various inboard and outdrive engine installations can be found in Pythons, up to a pair of 200hp Volvo diesels giving a top speed of over 25 knots.

Length overall	27ft 0in (8.23m)
Beam	12ft 0in (3.66m)
Draught	2ft 6in (0.76m)
Hull/deck material	GRP

SEAMASTER 8 METRE

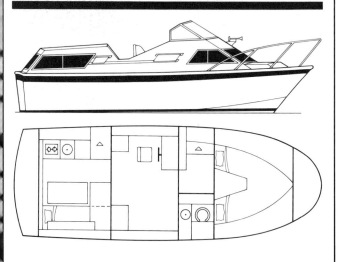

THE Seamaster 8 Metre was first built in 1970, last built in 1980. Builders Seamaster Ltd turned out 115 boats of this model, one of their extensive range of 20 to 30ft cruisers.

Breaking with convention, the boat has its main living area, with galley and dinette, in the aft cabin. The dinette can be converted into a double berth (that much is conventional), and there are two single berths in a forward cabin, ahead of the toilet compartment and a large wardrobe. In between the cabins, the helm position is in a midships cockpit, open but with a canopy that can give overhead shelter or, with side panels in place, can enclose the area completely.

The shallow to medium-vee hull has a long, shallow keel, making the boat suitable for inland or coastal cruising. Powered by single or twin BMC, Ford or Perkins diesels, usually of about 50hp, the boat is capable of 12 to 13 knots.

Length overall	27ft 0in (8.23m)
Beam	10ft 5in (3.18m)
Draught	2ft 3in (0.69m)
Hull/deck material	GRP

SELCRUISER 27

THE Selcruiser 27 dates from 1963. This fast cruiser was built by Selco of Norway and was originally imported by Carl Ziegler Yacht Agency. When those other well-known Norwegian motorboat builders, Fjord Plast, took over Selco in 1972 they incorporated the boat into their range, adding an aft cabin, amongst several modifications, and renaming it the Fjordcruiser 27. Fjords were imported at that time by J G Meakes. Altogether over 200 Selcruisers and Fjordcruisers were sold in the UK, up to 1978.

The Selcruiser (illustrated) has four berths in an open-plan cabin while the Fjordcruiser has five, two in the aforementioned aft cabin and three in a slightly smaller main cabin. Both boats have an open cockpit and helm position.

Hull shape is medium-vee. Selco fitted a pair of 110hp Volvo petrol outdrives, giving a top speed of about 20 knots. Fjordcruisers are mostly powered by single Volvo outdrives — a 106hp diesel (12 to 13 knots) or a 170hp petrol engine (about 17 knots).

Length overall	27ft 0in (8.23m)
Beam	9ft 10in (3.00m)
Draught	2ft 8in (0.81m)
Hull/deck material	GRP

OMEGA 828

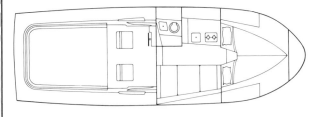

BACK in the mid-1960s there was an express cruiser called the Corsair, which was designed by Renato Levi and built by Viking Marine. Only a dozen or so were produced, and the hull mould was later bought by Trident Marine. They built a new mould, retaining the deep-vee underwater sections but giving the boat an added upper chine and redesigned topsides, and they called the boats that emerged from it the Omega 828. Between 1972 and 1978, 28 Omega 828s were built. Despite the un-Levi-like flare in the bows, the boat still has the designer's features of a very deep vee hull and a marked reverse sheer, and like the genuine Levis has a reputation as a good, fast sea boat.

The boat sleeps four, on two vee berths forward and a convertible dinette. There is an open helm position in a very large cockpit.

The first 10 boats were fitted with two 180hp Ford Mermaid diesel inboards, most of the rest with a pair of the Sabre versions of the same engine. A couple were given twin 170hp Volvo diesel outdrives. Top speed with any of these installations should be between 30 and 34 knots.

Length overall	27ft 6in (8.38m)
Beam	9ft 6in (2.90m)
Draught	2ft 10in (0.86m)
Hull/deck material	GRP

CLEOPATRA 850

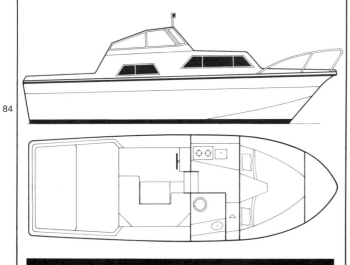

Length overall	27ft 10in (8.48m)
Beam	9ft 4in (2.84m)
Draught	2ft 7in (0.79m)
Hull/deck material	GRP

ESSEX Yacht Builders launched the Cleopatra 850 in 1970 and they and their successors, Eastwood Marine and Cleopatra Cruisers, built about 350 boats up to 1985. There are three versions of the boat: the standard version called the Family Cruiser; the International (illustrated), which has an outside helm only, on a bridge deck; and the Sportsrider, which has a large cockpit and less accommodation.

The Family Cruiser has four berths — two in the forward cabin and two in the wheelhouse/saloon. The International has five berths, with an additional berth in what is, in this version, a pure deck saloon. The Sportsrider has two berths in a forward cabin, and has an outdside, cockpit helm position.

Hull shape is shallow to medium-vee. The standard and most common engine installation is a pair of 130hp petrol Volvos, driving through outdrives and giving a top speed of about 25 knots.

SUNSEEKER 28

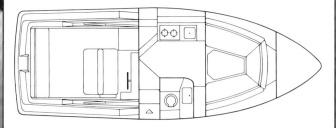

LAUNCHED in 1979, the 28 Offshore was the first of the Sunseeker range of sports cruisers and weekenders to be designed by Don Shead — he has been responsible for all new Sunseekers since then. Poole Powerboats (now known as Sunseeker International) built 136 examples up to 1986.

The boat has accommodation for four, with two berths in the saloon and two in a mini cabin protruding under the forward, raised part of the cockpit. In the cockpit there's seating for seven or eight and the aft seat can be converted into a large sunbed.

As on all the Sunseekers, hull shape is deep-vee. Power comes from twin petrol or diesel outdrives, the most popular installations being 200 or 260hp Volvo petrol engines, giving top speeds of up to 34 and 38 knots respectively, and 165hp Volvo diesels, which should give up to 32 knots.

The Sunseeker 28 Portofino is a dayboat/weekender version of the boat, with more cockpit and less (only two-berth) accommodation.

Length overall	27ft 10n (8.48m)
Beam	9ft 10in (3.00m)
Draught	2ft 0in (0.61m)
Hull/deck material	GRP

COLVIC 28

COLVIC Craft introduced their Colvic 28 motor cruiser hull and deck mouldings in 1976, but the design dates from 1965; the medium-vee hull is basically the same as that of the Tod Tornado. Colvic 28s were fitted out by other yards and a few by DIY owners. Severn Valley Cruisers produced several under the name of **Severn Traveller**. Whitfield Marine fitted out a few which they called the **Whitfield 28**. Altogether about 250 boats were built. Production ended in 1987.

Interior fitting out varies within the two basic layouts of aft-cabin and aft-cockpit versions, the former usually with six berths, the latter with four. Both versions have an open-backed wheelhouse.

Engine installations vary enormously, from single diesel inboards of as little as 30hp — for river use — to twin 170hp petrol outdrives, giving top speeds of over 20 knots.

Length overall	28ft 0in (8.53m)
Beam	9ft 6in (2.90m)
Draught	2ft 6in (0.76m)
Hull/deck material	GRP

FAIRLINE 29 MIRAGE

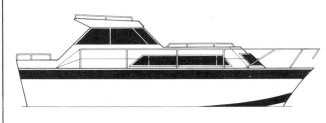

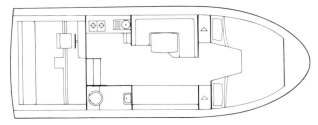

Length overall	28ft 5in (8.66m)
Beam	10ft 1in (3.07m)
Draught	2ft 0in (0.61m)
Hull/deck material	GRP

IN an 11-year production run, from 1975 to 1986, Fairline Boats produced 528 Fairline Mirage 29s. The boat was designed by John Bennett.

There is accommodation for five — two in a forward cabin and three in the saloon, which has a dinette convertible into a double berth and a settee-cum-single berth. The helm position is in a wheelhouse open to a small aft cockpit, which has a settee that can be pulled out into a sunbed.

The hull is medium-vee with a shallow, three-quarter-length keel. The most popular of a large range of Volvo outdrive options — single or twin, diesel or petrol — was a pair of 140hp petrol engines, giving 26 to 29 knots.

FAIRLINE 29 MIRAGE AC

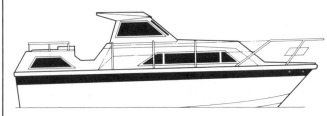

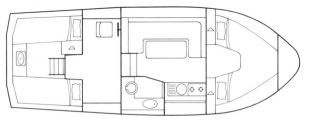

Length overall	28ft 6in (8.69m)
Beam	10ft 2in (3.10m)
Draught	2ft 9in (0.84m)
Hull/deck material	GRP

ALTHOUGH based on the same hull as the 29 Mirage, the Fairline 29 Mirage Aft Cabin is a very different boat, not just in accommodation layout but in engine installation and in the market it was aimed at; it is primarily a river boat, though quite capable of coastal cruising. Fairline Boats built 80 Mirage Aft Cabins, between 1981 and 1984.

The boat has six berths: two in the saloon, which is smaller than on the Mirage, two in the forward cabin and two in the aft cabin. On some boats the midships cockpit is open, but most have an open-backed wheelhouse.

Power comes from single or twin diesel inboards. A pair of 36hp Volvos, as commonly fitted, should give a top speed of about 10 knots.

RELCRAFT 29

RELIANCE Marine introduced the Relcraft 29 in 1976 and built about 200 up to 1981. There were two versions of this fast cruiser: the Zircon, with centre cockpit and aft cabin, and the Topaz, without the aft cabin but with a very large cockpit.

The Zircon sleeps six, with four berths in an open-plan forward cabin and two in the aft cabin. The Topaz sleeps four, with just the open-plan forward cabin. Both boats have a hard top over the helm position. The photograph and drawings show the Zircon.

Like the other boats in the Relcraft range the hull, designed by John Moxham, is deep vee with concave chines. Power comes from single or twin outdrives, commonly twin petrol Mercruisers or Volvos of 120 or 140hp each, the latter pushing the boat along at up to 25 knots.

Length overall	28ft 6in (8.69m)
Beam	9ft 6in (2.90m)
Draught	2ft 6in (0.76m)
Hull/deck material	GRP

TOD TORNADO

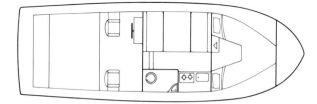

W & J Tod, of Weymouth, launched the Tod Tornado in 1962 and built 60 up to 1970. The boat was advertised as a cruiser/racer and several did compete in offshore powerboat events, including one in the Round Britain Race in 1969.

In standard form the boat sleeps four in an open-plan cabin, with a separate toilet compartment. The helm position is open in most boats, though some have been fitted with a hard top. A few boats were built with additional accommodation in an aft cabin.

Hull shape is shallow-vee. Various twin-engine installations were fitted to the boats, the majority being conventional-drive petrol or diesel inboards, though some had Volvo outdrive petrol engines. The most popular installation was a pair of 145hp Perkins diesel inboards, which pushed the boat along at up to 30 knots.

Length overall	28ft 6in (8.69m)
Beam	9ft 6in (2.90m)
Draught	2ft 9in (0.84m)
Hull/deck material	GRP

FAIREY HUNTSMAN 28

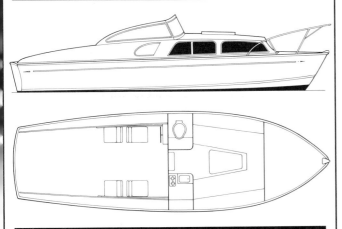

THE Fairey Huntsman 28 is the classic boat of its time, an express cruiser but famous for its achievements in racing. Huntsman 28s took part in every Cowes-Torquay race in the 1960s, including the first one in 1961, in which *Diesel Huntsman* came third, and in the 1969 Round Britain Race, in which they finished 3rd, 5th, 6th and 12th.

Based on the deep-vee hull design pioneered by American Ray Hunt, the boat was built by Fairey Marine on the Hamble River, of hot-moulded timber construction, using layers of agba veneer. Between 1960 and 1972, 144 Huntsman 28s were built.

Half the length of the boat is taken up by a vast cockpit. In the standard version the cabin has just two berths but some boats were built with a double child's berth right forward, and in a few the backs of the settees could be hinged up to form two bunk berths.

Most boats were fitted with twin diesels, early ones with 95 or 105hp Ford Parsons (top speed 22 to 24 knots). From 1964 onwards 135 or 145hp Perkins (28 to 30 knots) were standard. Some later boats were fitted with 175hp Ford Sabres or Mermaids (33 knots).

Length overall	28ft 10in (8.79m)
Beam	8ft 9in (2.67m)
Draught	2ft 6in (0.76m)
Hull/deck material	wood

BIRCHWOOD 29

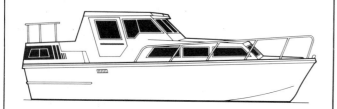

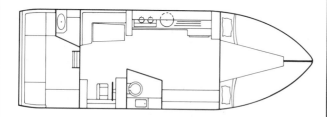

THE BIRCHWOOD 29 was introduced by the Birchwood Boat Co in 1976 and was in production until 1983, by which time over 200 had been built. The boat was sold in two versions, one with an aft cabin (illustrated) and one without.

There are four berths in the forward accommodation and a settee which can be used as a single in the enclosed wheelhouse. The aft cabin option gives another two berths.

The hull is medium-vee with a three-quarter-length keel. Various single and twin, diesel and petrol inboard installations were fitted. With a pair of 170hp Volvo or BMW petrol engines, the boat's top speed would be between 20 and 23 knots.

Length overall	29ft 1in (8.86m)
Beam	10ft 5in (3.18m)
Draught	3ft 0in (0.91m)
Hull/deck material	GRP

OCEAN 30

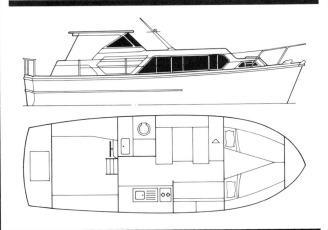

AQUA-FIBRE moulded the hull and superstructure of the Ocean 30 for other yards, and some individuals, to fit out. This round-bilged displacement cruiser was in production from 1966 to 1979. Herbert Woods were the predominant fitters-out until 1975, R A Nunn after that. Between 1968 and 1970 Bell-Buxton produced the **Moonraker 30** based on the Ocean 30 hull. Over 100 Ocean 30s, and about 40 Moonraker 30s, were built. Most can be found on rivers but the boats are quite capable of seagoing, at least in their twin-engine form.

Each boat features one of three accommodation layouts. Some have just four berths (two-berth cabin forward and dinette-cum-double berth in the saloon) and a large aft cockpit; some have an additional single cabin aft to starboard; and some have a double aft cabin. The helm position is basically open, though many boats have a hardtop to give some shelter from the elements.

Power is provided by single or twin 42hp Mercedes diesels, giving speeds of about 9 or 11 knots respectively.

Length overall	29ft 9in (9.07m)
Beam	10ft 2in (3.10m)
Draught	2ft 6in (0.76m)
Hull/deck material	GRP

BROOM 30

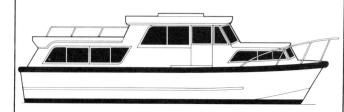

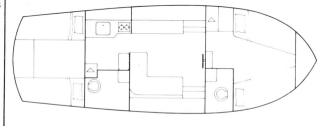

BASED on the hull of the Ocean 30, the Broom 30 was fitted out by C J Broom & Sons of Brundall, Norfolk, who completed 250 boats between 1966 and 1981. Most Broom 30s are used on rivers but some twin-engined versions have successfully cruised across the North Sea and English Channel to the Continental waterways. Early boats have a wooden superstructure but an all-GRP version was introduced in 1968.

With a longer and higher superstructure than the Ocean 30, the accommodation is considerably more generous. There are two berths in a spacious aft cabin, two in the forecabin and a settee-cum-double in the enclosed wheelhouse/saloon (which has a sunroof). There's also the luxury of two toilet compartments. For the upper reaches of the Thames, and some other rivers, Broom produced a version with a collapsible wheelhouse called the Broom Skipper.

The boats are generally powered by Perkins diesels, single or twin 35hp (45hp from 1969) or single 70hp. Top speed with one 35/45hp engine is 8½ knots, with two 50s or one 70hp 9½ knots.

Length overall	30ft 0in (9.14m)
Beam	10ft 4in (3.15m)
Draught	2ft 6in (0.76m)
Hull/deck material	GRP/wood or GRP

FAIREY SPEARFISH

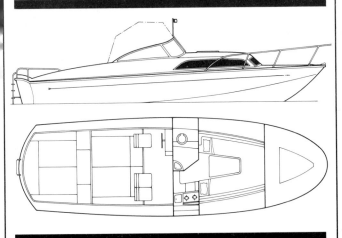

Length overall	30ft 0in (9.14m)
Beam	9ft 6in (2.90m)
Draught	2ft 9in (0.84m)
Hull/deck material	GRP

IN essence a GRP version of the Fairey Huntsman 31, the Fairey Spearfish was launched by Fairey Marine in 1971. About 200 were built (including 25 for Colonel Gadafi, the Libyan leader), the last ones in 1976. The first two boats were built with marine-ply superstructures but the rest have GRP tops and bottoms.

It is the aft cockpit version of the Huntsman that the Spearfish resembles, with the accent on dayboating space in a very large cockpit and just two berths, a simple galley and a separate toilet compartment, in the small cabin.

Early boats are powered by twin 145hp Perkins or 150hp Ford Mermaid diesels, and have a top speed of 28 to 29 knots. Later boats are most commonly powered by a pair of 180 or 210hp Ford Sabres or Mermaids (31 knots or 33 knots respectively).

FREEMAN 30

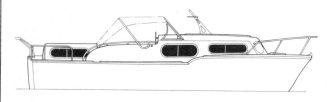

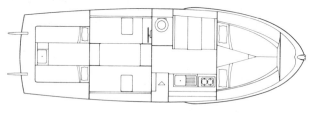

JOHN Freeman (Marine) built about 100 Freeman 30s from 1960 to 1969. The boat has the distinctive curved step in the deck line that was a feature of many of the early Freemans. The first 30s were built with wooden (mahogany) deck and superstructure; later examples were all GRP.

There are two versions, one with a centre cockpit and aft cabin and one with an aft cockpit. The centre-cockpit version has six berths, the other has four. The photograph and drawings show the GRP, aft-cabin boat.

Hull form is shallow-vee with a long, shallow keel. The boats were primarily built for river use but are capable of fair-weather passages in estuarial or coastal waters.

Single or twin diesels were fitted. In the early boats the most common installations are a pair of 56hp Parsons Porbeagles, which would give a top speed of 9 to 10 knots. Later boats were fitted with more powerful engines, commonly a pair of 108hp Thornycrofts, which would increase top speed to 12 to 13 knots.

Length overall	30ft 0in (9.14m)
Beam	10ft 6in (3.20m)
Draught	2ft 6in (0.76m)
Hull/deck material	GRP/wood or GRP

SEAMASTER 30

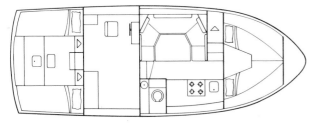

Length overall	30ft 0in (9.14m)
Beam	11ft 6in (3.51m)
Draught	2ft 9in (0.84m)
Hull/deck material	GRP

SEAMASTER, a famous name in motorboat building in the 1960s and '70s, launched the Seamaster 30 at the 1970 London Boat Show, and produced 410 of the model up to 1981. The hull and superstructure moulds are held by Viking Mouldings, who occupy the old Seamaster premises in Great Dunmow, Essex.

The boat sleeps six, with two berths in a forward cabin, two in the saloon and two in an aft cabin. Helm position is in an open-backed midships wheelhouse.

Hull shape is shallow-vee with a three-quarter-length, shallow keel. Standard engine installation is a pair of 50hp Thornycroft diesels but several others — all twins — were also fitted, including 50hp Perkins diesels. Top speed with Thornycrofts or Perkins should be 12 to 13 knots.

ANCAS QUEEN SELQUEEN 30

Length overall	30ft 2in (9.19m)
Beam	10ft 8in (3.25m)
Draught	2ft 3in (0.69m)
Hull/deck material	GRP

THOMAS Nelson Yachts introduced the Ancas Queen 30 into the UK in 1967. This Norwegian-built fast cruiser was designed by Ray Hunt of the USA and sports a typical Hunt constant-deadrise, deep-vee hull. In 1970, following the takeover of Ancas by Selco, the boat became the Selqueen 30. About 30 Ancas Queen and Selqueen 30s were imported into the UK, up to 1972.

There's accommodation for four in an unusual layout. The two forward berths are enclosed within a cabin whose top is just below window level, so you only have sitting headroom in it. But in the main cabin you have the benefit of the light and view through the forward windows, and a very large shelf. The main cabin has a settee which can be pulled out into a double berth. There is an open helm position in a large aft cockpit.

Power comes from twin outdrive engines. Various makes and powers were fitted, from 130hp Volvos to 210hp Chrysler petrol engines, the latter giving a top sped of over 30 knots. A few are powered by twin 92hp Volvo diesels.

PRINCESS 30DS

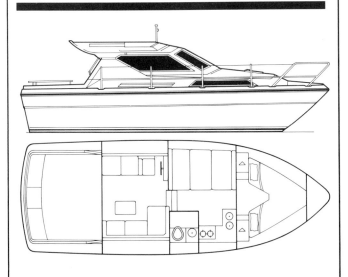

Length overall	30ft 5in (9.27m)
Beam	11ft 0in (3.35m)
Draught	2ft 11in (0.89m)
Hull/deck material	GRP

MARINE Projects launched the Princess 30DS at the 1980 Southampton Boat Show, and built around 900 up to 1989.

There are six berths — two in the deck saloon (that's what DS stands for), two in the lower saloon (a convertible dinette) and two in a separate forward cabin. The deck saloon doubles as wheelhouse and has a large sunroof (except on boats built with the flying bridge option, available from 1986). Sliding glass doors lead out from the wheelhouse/saloon to an aft cockpit.

Designed by Bernard Olesinski, the boat has a semi deep-vee hull (deep-vee at midships, medium-vee aft) and a reputation for good seakeeping at planing speeds. A great variety of engines have been fitted — single and twin, inboard and outdrive, petrol and diesel. Most common are two 145hp Volvo petrol outdrives or a pair of 130hp Volvo inboard diesels, both giving top speeds around the 25-knot mark.

ROYAL 31

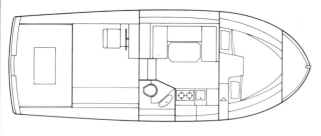

INTRODUCED in 1977, the Royal 31 is still in production. To date the Swedish builders, Storebro Bruks, have exported over 100 of the boats into the UK.

The Royal 31 is really three different boats, based on the same hull and with the same engine options, but with three quite different layouts. The 31 Adriatic has a vast open cockpit and four berths. The 31 Baltic has an aft cabin, midships cockpit and open helm position and a total of six berths, while the 31 Biscay has an enclosed wheelhouse-cum-saloon, small aft cockpit and six berths, including a pull-out dougle in the wheelhouse/saloon. The Biscay (illustrated) and the Baltic have been by far the most popular models in the UK.

The boats are powered by twin Volvo diesels ranging from 240 to 384hp in total, with top speeds of between 18 and 27 knots. Like all Royals, the 31 has a semi-displacement hull and a reputation as a well-built, immaculately fitted out and seaworthy motor cruiser.

Length overall	30ft 6in (9.30m)
Beam	10ft 6in (3.20m)
Draught	3ft 1in (0.94m)
Hull/deck material	GRP

SUNSEEKER 31

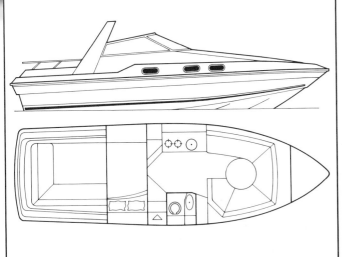

DESIGNED by Don Shead and built by Poole Powerboats (now Sunseeker International), the Sunseeker 31 Offshore sports cruiser was introduced in 1982 and remained in production until 1986, when it was replaced by the 31 Portofino, based on the same hull but with a redesigned layout. During that period, 123 boats were built.

The boat sleeps four, a large circular dinette area converting to a double berth (big enough in fact to sleep three or four) and a guest cabin having a double berth under the cockpit. In the standard layout the cockpit has a double helm seat and an L-shaped settee which will seat six or seven; the alternative layout has a vast cushioned sunlounger in place of the settee.

Hull shape is deep-vee. Power comes from a pair of petrol or diesel outdrives. Petrol installations include twin 200hp or 260hp Volvos, giving top speeds of about 30 and 34-35 knots respectively; diesel options include twin 135hp BMWs (24 knots) and 165hp Volvos (29-30 knots).

Length overall	30ft 10in (9.40m)
Beam	10ft 0in (3.05m)
Draught	2ft 0in (0.61m)
Hull/deck material	GRP

BERTRAM 31

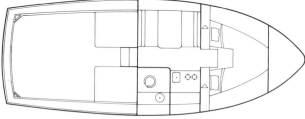

Length overall	31ft 0in (9.45m)
Beam	11ft 2in (3.40m)
Draught	2ft 4in (0.71m)
Hull/deck material	GRP

THE prototype of the Bertram 31 won the 1960 Miami-Nassau Powerboat Race in very rough seas and yet in record time, a result which launched not only the Bertram range of fast cruisers but the concept of the deep-vee hull, 'invented' by American naval architect Ray Hunt. The Bertram Yacht Company launched the production version of the 31 on the crest of the resulting publicity and have been building the boat, with some modifications, ever since. It has never been imported into the UK in vast numbers, but Thomas Nelson Yacht Agency brought in about 20 between 1962 and '66.

The Bertram 31 Express Cruiser was the most popular version of the boat on this side of the Atlantic in the mid-1960s. It has an open helm position in a very large aft cockpit, with four berths in the cabin in the now familiar arrangement of a dinette convertible into a double berth and two vee berths forward.

Standard engine installation in the '60s was a pair of 280hp Chrysler petrol inboards, which pushed the boat along at up to 30 knots.

BIRCHWOOD 31

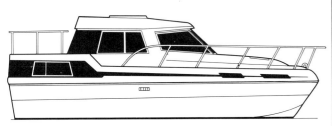

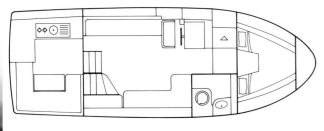

THE Birchwood 31 Commodore was only in production for three years, from 1981 to 1984, but nearly 100 boats emerged from Birchwood's Sutton-in-Ashfield factory during that short time.

In an unconventional layout, the standard boat has its main living area, with dinette and galley, in the aft cabin. The dinette converts into a double berth and there is a double in the forward cabin and two singles in the wheelhouse/saloon. Another version has a more conventional arrangement with galley and dinette forward of the wheelhouse. There are inside and outside helm positions, in the wheelhouse and on the raised aft deck.

The 31 is based on a hull designed by Graham Caddick, basically medium-vee in shape but with rounded sections forward — convex below the water line, concave above it — and a deepish three-quarter-length keel. Power comes from single or twin, diesel or petrol engines. Top speed with a pair of 138hp petrol Volvos or 145hp diesel Volvos should be about 20 knots.

Length overall	31ft 0in (9.45m)
Beam	11ft 0in (3.35m)
Draught	3ft 0in (0.91m)
Hull/deck material	GRP

CHRIS-CRAFT 31

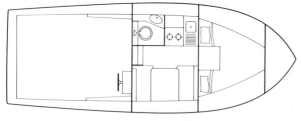

ALONG with the Chris-Craft 26, the 31 Commander was one of the cruisers imported during the mid-1960s by Carl Ziegler Yacht Agency from the long-established Chris-Craft Corporation of America. Unlike the 26, this one was actually built in the USA, in Florida. Between 20 and 30 came into the UK between 1964 and 1969.

The boat sleeps up to six people — two in a forward cabin and four in the saloon, which has a convertible dinette and settee which converts into two bunk berths. The standard boat has an open helm position in the cockpit but many have the optional hard top.

Hull shape is rather unusual, with concave sections giving an underwater shape that on average is somewhere between deep-vee (along the centreline) and shallow-vee (under the chine) and effectively gives a very shallow keel, which helps with low-speed directional stability. Most of the boats imported into the UK were fitted with twin 145hp horizontal Perkins diesels, which give a top speed of 22 to 23 knots.

Length overall	31ft 0in (9.45m)
Beam	11ft 3in (3.43m)
Draught	2ft 4in (0.71m)
Hull/deck material	GRP

RAPIER 3100

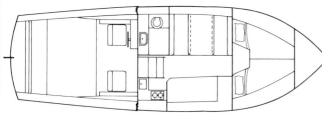

THE Rapier 3100 was designed by Cox & Haswell, and like the same designers' Pegasus 35, the boat is genuinely 'race-proven'. A standard Rapier, called (confusingly) *Pegasus*, took part in the 1967 Cowes-Torquay Powerboat Race and won the Index of Performance, Concours d'Elegance and Best All-Rounder Trophies, while finishing 25th overall. And like the Pegasus 35, a disappointingly small number of these excellent boats were built; the Christchurch Yacht Company launched just 12 Rapiers between 1966 and 1972. Construction was of cold-moulded mahogany with Cascover nylon hull sheathing.

The boats were built to a standard layout — large aft cockpit with a helm position that can be sheltered with an overhead canopy, and four berths in an open-plan cabin.

Hull shape is moderate-vee, with a fine entry. Engines are twin 145hp Perkins inboard diesels, giving a top speed of around 30 knots.

Length overall	31ft 0in (9.45m)
Beam	10ft 3in (3.12m)
Draught	2ft 6in (0.76m)
Hull/deck material	wood

SENIOR 31

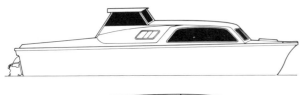

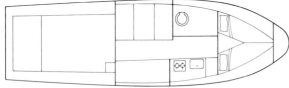

Length overall	31ft 0in (9.45m)
Beam	9ft 8in (2.95m)
Draught	1ft 3in (0.38m)
Hull/deck material	GRP

THE most popular of the extraordinarily successful Senior range of motor cruisers, the Senior 31 was in production for nearly 20 years, from 1963 to 1982. Senior Marine of Southampton built about a thousand 31s, many of them sold as hull and superstructure mouldings for private individuals or other boatyards to fit out. The **RLM Entice 32**, which was produced by RLM Marine, was based on Senior 31 mouldings and so was Marine Projects' Project 31.

In the standard Senior Marine version there are five berths — two in a forward cabin and three in the saloon, including a dinette-cum-double berth — with a large aft cockpit and open-backed wheelhouse.

The hull is of semi-displacement form, basically round-bilge but with flattish shallow-vee sections aft, and a half-length shallow keel for low-speed directional stability. The most popular engine installation is a pair of 50hp Perkins diesel outdrives, which give a top speed of about 12 knots. Speeds of 16 to 17 knots are possible with, say, a pair of 75 or 80hp engines.

FAIREY HUNTSMAN 31

LIKE the Huntsman 28, the Fairey Huntsman 31 has a Ray Hunt-inspired deep-vee hull but with a slightly deeper vee and more overhang in the bow, making the boat softer-riding and drier than the 28. Fairey Marine built 31 of this model, between 1968 and 1973. Like their smaller sisters, Huntsman 31s competed regularly in Cowes-Torquay Powerboat races and one finished fourth in the 1969 Round Britain Race. Two took part in the London to Monte-Carlo Race in 1972, with mixed fortunes; one finished sixth, the other sank.

A few boats were fitted out in a similar layout to the 28, with a very large cockpit and two-berth cabin, but most have a midships cockpit and a further two berths in an aft cabin.

The original standard engine installation was a pair of 145hp Perkins diesels, driving the boat at up to 27 knots. From 1970 onwards most boats were fitted with twin 180hp or 210hp Ford Sabres or Ford Mermaids, giving top speeds of about 30 and 32-33 knots respectively.

Length overall	31ft 3in (9.53m)
Beam	9ft 8in (2.95m)
Draught	2ft 10in (0.86m)
Hull/deck material	wood

CORONET 32

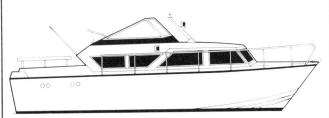

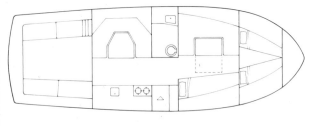

IN the late 1960s, and early mid '70s, Botved Boats of Denmark were one of the biggest production motorboat builders in Europe. In the UK the Coronet 32 Oceanfarer was the most popular of their range of cruisers, over 50 being imported between 1969 and 1978, by Dell Quay Sales until 1972 and then by Poole Powerboats (now Sunseeker International).

With an outside helm position on a kind of semi flying bridge the boat has a remarkably spacious interior, with sleeping accommodation for five adults and two children, a dinette-cum-double berth in the saloon and in the forecabin, three full-size berths and two small berths right forward on a higher level.

Hull shape is medium-vee. Engine installations include twin 145hp and (on later boats) 175hp Perkins diesels, with top speeds respectively of about 22 and 25 knots, and twin 170hp Volvo petrols, with a top speed of about 25 knots.

Length overall	32ft 0in (9.75m)
Beam	10ft 9in (3.28m)
Draught	2ft 6in (0.76m)
Hull/deck material	GRP

CORVETTE 32

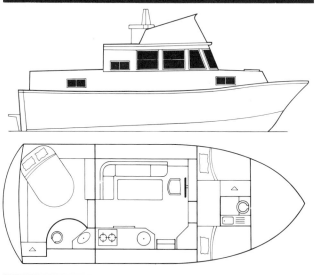

Length overall	32ft 0in (9.75m)
Beam	13ft 0in (3.96m)
Draught	4ft 0in (1.22m)
Hull/deck material	GRP

A TRAWLER yacht with a difference, the Corvette 32 is British-built, has a most unusual hull shape (round bilge sections flanked by shallow vee flats out to the chine) and is fast. The boat was designed by Compton, McGill and built, initially, by Corvette Marine, who produced about 30 between 1974 and 1977, when they went into liquidation. In 1984 the moulds were bought by a new company, Corvette Cruisers, who have redesigned the interior and built another 70 boats.

There is accommodation for six, including two in an aft cabin and two in the deck saloon-cum-wheelhouse. Main features of the exterior layout are wide side decks and a large flying bridge.

Most of the original boats are powered by twin 106hp Volvo diesel outdrives or 105hp Mercedes diesels working through V-drives. Top speed is 16 to 18 knots. Corvette Cruisers fit conventional-drive engines, most commonly two 210hp Cummins diesels, which give a top speed of 22 knots.

FREEMAN 32

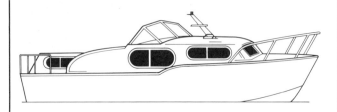

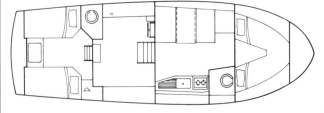

LAUNCHED in 1968, the Freeman 32 was another of the older-style cruisers from John Freeman (Marine), with rounded lines and, in the earlier models, the familiar step in the deckline. Over 100 were built up to 1975, when the Freeman 33 was introduced.

The boat sleeps six, with two berths in an aft cabin, two in the saloon (a convertible dinette) and two in a forward cabin. The earliest boats had an open, midships helm position but in 1972 the boat was restyled, losing the deckline step and gaining an open-backed wheelhouse. Later still the wheelhouse became fully enclosed.

The photograph and plan show one of the later models, the profile an earlier boat.

A shallow-vee hull, with a long shallow keel, makes the boat suitable both for low river speeds and for semi-displacement performance at sea. Twin diesel inboards of various powers — usually Ford or Thornycroft — were fitted. A pair of 108hp Thornycrofts should give a top speed of between 13 and 15 knots.

Length overall	32ft 0in (9.75m)
Beam	10ft 6in (3.20m)
Draught	2ft 9in (0.84m)
Hull/deck material	GRP

GRAND BANKS 32

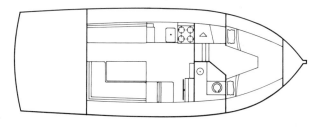

OVER 900 Grand Banks 32s have been built since this smallest of the Grand Banks range of trawler yachts was launched in 1965. Only about 30 have been imported into the UK. The boat was (and still is) built by American Marine, in Hong Kong until 1970 and in Singapore since then. Construction was in wood (mahogany planking and teak decks) until 1973, but has been in GRP since then. Grand Banks boats (32, 36 and 42) are amongst the best trawler yachts around, and the most expensive.

The GB32 has two berths forward and a settee which converts into a double berth in the spacious saloon/ wheelhouse, which also houses the galley. Outside, there's an aft cockpit and a large flying bridge.

The hard-chine hull form, with long keel, is designed primarily for displacement speeds. Power comes from a single Ford Lehman diesel of 120hp (pre-1984) or 135hp, giving top speeds of 8 knots and 9 to 10 knots respectively.

Length overall	32ft 0in (9.75m)
Beam	11ft 6in (3.51m)
Draught	3ft 9in (1.14m)
Hull/deck material	wood or GRP

RAMPART 32/36

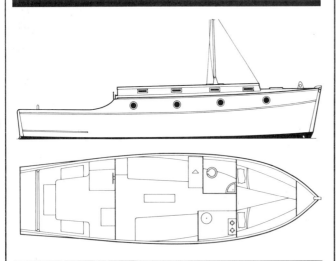

RAMPART Boatbuilding, of Southampton, were one of the last companies to be regularly building motor cruisers of conventional timber construction. The Rampart 32 (illustrated) and the Rampart 36, a development of the same displacement cruiser, date from 1952, but the last ones were not built until 1972. By modern standards the number built was not great — 25 boats of both lengths, and four similar 33-footers — but that was quite a significant number for a wooden boat. Hulls are mahogany planking on Canadian rock elm frames, with sheathed ply decks.

The accommodation is split into two cabins, with berths for four in the 32, and five in the 36. The helm position is in the cockpit or in an open-backed wheelhouse.

The 32 was fitted with a great variety of engines, most commonly single or twin Perkins and BMC diesels of 35 to 50hp, giving a top speed of about 9 knots. Nearly all the 36s have twin diesels — BMC Commodores (45 to 52hp) in most of the earlier boats, 72hp Perkins in the later ones, which have a top speed of 10 knots or just under.

	Rampart 32	Rampart 36
Length overall	32ft 0in (9.75m)	36ft 0in (10.97m)
Beam	9ft 3in (2.82m) ...	10ft 6in (3.20m)
Draught	2ft 9in (0.84m)	3ft 4in (1.10m)
Hull/deck material	wood	wood

SENIOR 32 SHEERLINE

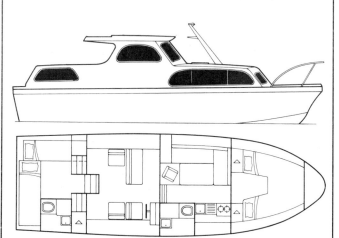

THE Senior 32 Sheerline, introduced in 1969, was based on the offshore powerboat *Translucent*, which competed in the 1969 and 1970 Cowes-Torquay races and the 1969 Round Britain race, in which she finished 11th overall. Senior Marine built about 100 examples up to 1978, and the design was kept alive until 1982 by RLM Marine. They produced their own version of the boat, called the RLM Riviera 33, from Sheerline hulls.

The boat sleeps six, with two berths in an aft cabin, two right forward and two, in the form of a convertible dinette, in the saloon. You drive the boat from inside an open-backed wheelhouse.

Hull shape is medium-vee. Various single and twin diesel inboard installations were fitted, up to a pair of 180hp Ford Sabres, which would give a top speed of over 25 knots.

Length overall	32ft 0in (9.75m)
Beam	10ft 1in (3.07m)
Draught	3ft 0in (0.91m)
Hull/deck material	GRP

WEYMOUTH 32

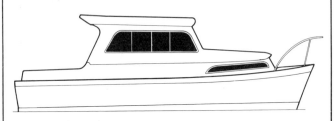

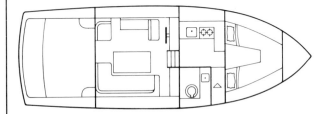

Length overall	32ft 0in (9.75m)
Beam	10ft 10in (3.30m)
Draught	2ft 9in (0.84m)
Hull/deck material	GRP or GRP/wood

JOHN Askham designed the Weymouth 32 for James & Caddy, of Weymouth, who built the first of these sturdy semi-displacement cruisers in 1969, based on a GRP hull moulded by Halmatic. About 20 were built between then and 1974, when the similar but slightly larger Weymouth 34 was introduced. The first 32s had a wooden deck and superstructure, but from 1972 most were all-GRP.

The boat was built in two versions, with either an aft cockpit or an aft cabin. Both had four berths, the aft-cockpit version with two of them in a slightly larger wheelhouse/saloon.

Hull shape is round-bilge with flattish sections aft. The standard engine installation is a pair of 145hp Perkins diesels, giving a top speed of between 18 and 20 knots.

FAIRLINE 32 PHANTOM

ALTHOUGH it doesn't look quite so radical as the original Fairline Fury, the Fairline 32 Phantom sports a similar, low-profile flying bridge, well forward and recessed into the superstructure; again it's the only helm position, resulting in a spacious and uncluttered accommodation. And again the boat was designed by John Bennett. Fairline Boats launched the Phantom in 1974 and built 310 of them, up to 1982.

The accommodation is split into two cabins, the after one being the main dining area with a dinette, which converts into a double berth, and the galley. The forward cabin has another dinette-cum-double berth, a settee-cum-single and, right forward, another berth that can be used as a single, athwartships, or by two small children. All this and a largish aft cockpit.

Hull shape is medium-vee with a three-quarter length keel. Most Phantoms were fitted with twin outdrives. One of the most popular installations was a pair of 165hp Volvo diesels, giving a top speed of 27 to 30 knots.

Length overall	32ft 2in (9.81m)
Beam	10ft 10in (3.30m)
Draught	2ft 0in (0.61m)
Hull/deck material	GRP

FAIRLINE 32 SEDAN

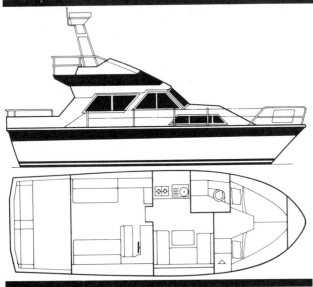

Length overall 32ft 2in (9.81m)
Beam 10ft 10in (3.30m)
Draught 2ft 0in (0.61m)
Hull/deck material .... GRP

BASED on the same hull as the 32 Phantom but with a completely redesigned deck and superstructure, the Fairline 32 Sedan is a conventional flying bridge fast cruiser. Fairline Boats launched the Sedan in 1976 and built 157 of them, up to 1984.

There is accommodation for six, with two berths in the forward cabin, two in the main saloon (from a convertible dinette) and two settees which can be used as single berths in the wheelhouse-cum-deck saloon.

Sedans were fitted with a wide range of Volvo outdrive engine installations — single and twin, diesel and petrol, most commonly a pair of 130hp Volvo diesels, giving a top speed of about 25 knots.

PROJECT 31

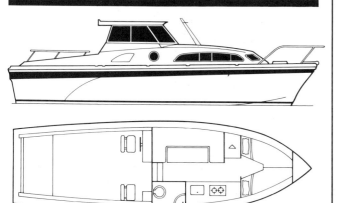

Length overall	32ft 2in (9.81m)
Beam	9ft 10in (3.00m)
Draught	2ft 9in (0.84m)
Hull/deck material	GRP

THIS is the boat that launched Marine Projects of Plymouth, now famous for their Princess range of motor cruisers. About 200 Project 31s were built betwen 1966 and 1974, based on the popular Senior 31 hull and superstructure.

The boat has a large cockpit and open-backed wheelhouse, with accommodation for four in a basically open-plan cabin, but with a folding partition and curtains giving optional privacy to the vee berths forward. A settee in the cockpit can be pulled out to form an additional fair-weather, under-the-canopy double berth.

The round-bilge hull form is capable of semi-displacement speeds, up to 16 or 17 knots with, for instance, a pair of 75hp Volvo outdrive diesels, or in a few cases about 20 knots with two 130hp petrol engines. But most boats were fitted with less powerful engines, such as a pair of 45hp Perkins diesels (driving through outdrives again), giving a top speed of about 12 knots.

PRINCESS 32

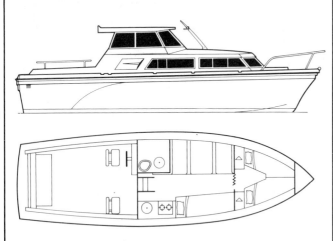

THE first Marine Projects boat to bear the now familiar name of Princess, the 32 was launched in 1969 and over 2000 were built from then until 1980. The boat was based on the Senior 31 hull, like the Project 31, with a modified transom and a completely different superstructure.

The layout is also similar to the Project 31 in having a large cockpit and open-backed wheelhouse and an interior that is basically open-plan but with a folding partition to isolate the two vee berths forward. However, there are five berths rather than four, with an additional single opposite the convertible dinette.

Marine Projects offered a wide choice of engine installations, all outdrives but either single or twin, diesel or petrol, and ranging in power from 75hp to 2 × 140hp. The smaller engines give a top speed of only about 10 knots with single installations, or 18 to 20 with twins, while a pair of 140s should give 25 knots or more.

Length overall	32ft 3in (9.83m)
Beam	10ft 0in (3.04m)
Draught	2ft 9in (0.84m)
Hull/deck material	GRP

AQUA STAR 32/33

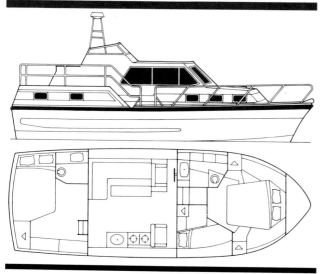

THE Aqua-Star 32 was introduced in 1972 and its successor, the 33, based on the same round-bilge, semi-displacement hull in 1980. The 33 is still in production. Aqua-Star Ltd have built over 900 of these models in total, about half as motor cruisers and half as commercial craft.

Like the Aqua-Star 27, the 32 and 33 appear in various versions. The Fast Sports Fisherman 32 and Sports Ranger 33 have large aft cockpits and four-berth accommodation. The Passagemaker 32 has a midships wheelhouse/saloon and six berths, including two in an aft cabin. The Searanger 32 has an extended wheelhouse-cum-deck saloon and an aft cockpit, and some were built with a flying bridge. The Oceanranger 33 has been built in aft cockpit and (post 1984) aft cabin versions, with six and eight berths respectively.

Power comes from a variety of inboard diesels, from 1 × 120hp (with a top speed of around 12 knots), to 2 × 180hp (nearly 25 knots).

The photograph shows a Sports Ranger 33, the drawings an Oceanranger 33.

	Aqua-Star 32	Aqua-Star 33
Length overall	32ft 4in (9.85m)	33ft 0in (10.05m)
Beam	11ft 6in (3.51m)	11ft 6in (3.51m)
Draught	3ft 0in (0.91m)	3ft 0in (0.91m)
Hull/deck material	GRP	GRP

LAGUNA 10M/11.5M

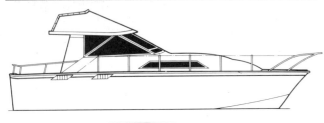

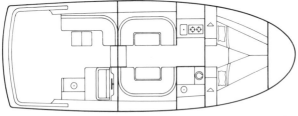

	10-Metre	11.5-Metre
Length overall	32ft 9in (9.98m)	37ft 9in (11.51m)
Beam	11ft 9in (3.58m)	14ft 5in (4.39)
Draught	2ft 3in (0.69m)	3ft 0in (0.91m)
Hull/deck material	GRP	GRP

IN THE early 1970s American Marine of Singapore, builders of the Grand Banks trawler yachts, built two versions of a fast motor yacht, the Laguna. They turned out about 100 of the 10-Metre (illustrated) and 50 of the 11.5-Metre, of which 17 and 13 respectively were imported into the UK, between 1970 and 1974.

The Laguna's sedan layout — aft-cockpit with a flying bridge on top of a wheelhouse featuring large sliding glass doors — is common enough today, but in the early 1970s it was decidedly novel. Interior layout was also unusual. Both boats can sleep up to eight people — in something of a squash on the 10-Metre. The 11.5-Metre's large saloon/wheelhouse contains two comfortable dinettes and the galley, while the 10-Metre has two galleys, the main one below and a secondary one in the wheelhouse.

Hull shape is medium-vee with a shallow keel. Both boats were fitted with a pair of 270hp GM diesels, giving top speeds of 27 knots in the 10-Metre and 22 knots in the 11.5-Metre.

CLEOPATRA 1000/33

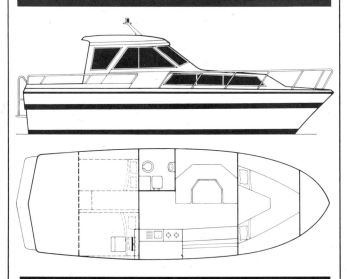

THIS fast cruiser was launched in 1971 as the Cleopatra 1000, but in 1973 was demetricated to become known as the Cleopatra 33. It was designed by Pelle Petersen of Sweden and built by Essex Yacht builders of Wallasea Island, on the Crouch, and by their successors, Eastwood Marine and Cleopatra Cruisers. About 230 boats were built, up to 1987.

The boat has an unusual interior layout and an unusually large number of berths. Up to eight people can sleep aboard, although that would include four people in the small cabin that runs from the saloon under the cockpit, with two double berths and standing headroom in between under a trunk coachroof. Two can sleep in the saloon, which has a convertible dinette, and two more in the forward cabin. The standard boat has an open-backed wheelhouse, but there are also enclosed wheelhouse (with or without flying bridge) and open-cockpit versions.

Length overall	33ft 0in (10.06m)
Beam	12ft 3in (3.73m)
Draught	4ft 0in (1.22m)
Hull/deck material	GRP

COBRA 33

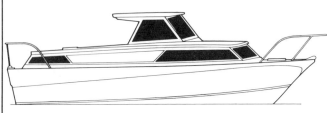

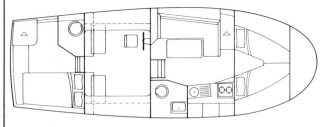

Length overall	33ft 0in (10.06m)
Beam	12ft 0in (3.66m)
Draught	2ft 6in (0.76m)
Hull/deck material	GRP

TOUGH Bros of Teddington built about 40 Cobra 33s, a stretched version of their Python 27, between 1970 and 1977, and like the Python the Cobra is still technically in production — Tough's still have the moulds and would build if they had the orders.

There is a sports-fishing version (large cockpit, two berths), a four-berth cruiser version (four berths in an open-plan forward cabin) and a six-berth cruiser (with aft cabin). All three have open-backed wheelhouses.

The boat, which has a deep-vee hull, was designed around a pair of the horizontal Perkins HT6.354 (145hp) diesels, which drive the boat at up to 25 knots. Various Ford diesel marinisations were also fitted, up to 2 × 200hp. A pair of 180hp Fords should give a top speed of 27 to 28 knots.

FAIREY SWORDSMAN

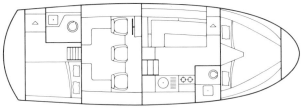

Length overall	33ft 0in (10.06m)
Beam	11ft 5in (3.48m)
Draught	3ft 0in (0.91m)
Hull/deck material	wood

FAIREY Marine, of Hamble, Hampshire, built just under 60 Fairey Swordsmans, between 1964 and 1974. The boat is a development of the Huntsman 31 express cruiser but with more emphasis on accommodation, less on cockpit space.

The main cabin has four berths, and most Swordsmans were built with an aft cabin, which brings the total sleeping capacity up to six. On earlier boats the aft cabin was a low-level affair, below the line of the cockpit coaming, but in 1972, in an updated version they called the Super Swordsman, Fairey Marine raised the cabin to give it standing headroom, and enlarged it to provide a second toilet compartment.

A pair of Perkins 136hp (later 145hp) diesel inboards was the original standard installation, giving a top speed of about 23 knots. Later boats are mostly powered by twin 180hp or 210hp Ford Sabres or Mermaids (26 or 28 knots). Some Swordsmans have been re-engined with 250hp Sabres, and can reach up to 31 knots.

FREEMAN 33

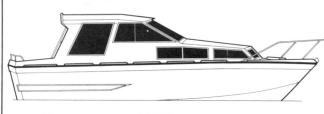

JOHN Freeman (Marine) launched their Freeman 33 in 1974 and produced about 150 boats before they finished boatbuilding in 1984.

There were four different versions of the boat, all with six berths. The Sedan version (illustrated) has an enclosed wheelhouse and aft cockpit, the Sport has a midships cockpit with open-backed wheelhouse and aft cabin and the Tobago (introduced in 1982) is a flying-bridge version of the Sedan.

The boat has a medium-vee hull with three-quarter-length shallow keel. Most boats were fitted with twin diesel inboard engines of between 120 and 230hp each, usually Ford Sabres or Volvos. A pair of 212hp Ford Sabres should give a top speed of 27 to 30 knots.

Length overall	33ft 0in (10.06m)
Beam	11ft 6in (3.51m)
Draught	2ft 8in (0.81m)
Hull/deck material	GRP

NORSEMAN 33/38

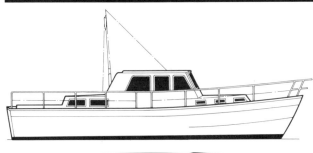

	Norseman 33	Norseman 38
Length overall	33ft 0in (10.06m)	38ft 0in (11.58m)
Beam	10ft 0in (3.05m)	11ft 3in (3.43)
Draught	3ft 9in (1.14m)	4ft 0in (1.22m)
Hull/deck material	GRP	GRP

BASED on the hulls of Viking Marine cruise liner tenders, turned into handsome round-bilge displacement cruisers by Scottish naval architects G L Watson & Co, the Norseman 33 and 38 were moulded by Viking and fitted out by Aberdour Marine and other yards, and also by many DIY owners. Altogether about 60 Norseman 33s and 40 Norseman 38s were built, between 1965 and 1974. The photograph is of a 33. The drawings show a 38.

All the boats had a midships wheelhouse with the main accommodation forward and a two-berth aft cabin. But otherwise layouts varied greatly, offering four to five berths in the 33, five to six in the 38. Some boats were built with a ketch rig to give a modest motor sailing capability; others had a simple mizzen mast to carry a steadying sail.

Most boats were fitted with twin diesels, commonly Thornycrofts or Newages of between 30 and 85hp each in the 33s, and between 60 and 100hp in 38s. Top speeds would be between 8 and 10 knots.

PRINCESS 33

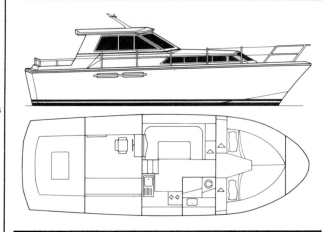

Length overall	33ft 0in (10.06m)
Beam	11ft 3in (3.43m)
Draught	3ft 0in (0.91m)
Hull/deck material	GRP

DESIGNED by John Bennett, Marine Projects' Princess 33 was in production from 1975 to 1987; nearly 500 were built.

The standard layout has six berths — two vee berths in a forward cabin, a convertible dinette/double in the lower saloon, and a settee which converts into a double berth in the wheelhouse-cum-deck saloon.

The most interesting feature of the 33 was the choice offered to purchasers of deep-vee or 'Y'-shaped hulls. The latter, with flatter sections aft and a long shallow keel, was intended for displacement and semi-displacement speeds. Various types and sizes of engines were fitted. Probably the most popular option was a pair of 80hp Ford inboard diesels, giving a top speed of 13 knots. The deep-vee version was for full planing performance. With two 130hp Ford diesels the boat should reach 17 to 18 knots. Some deep vee versions have a flying bridge.

The Y'-shaped hull was phased out with the arrival of a Mk2 version in 1981, which had a modified superstructure with an extra settee which could be used as a seventh berth, plus a standard flying bridge.

PROFILE 33

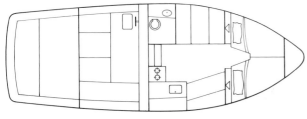

Length overall	33ft 0n (10.06m)
Beam	11ft 0in (3.35m)
Draught	2ft 9in (0.84m)
Hull/deck material	GRP

THE Profile 33 is unusual in being a modern displacement cruiser, a round-bilge boat with a top speed of under 10 knots. Dave Gannaway designed the boat and 76 of them were built by Profile Marine of Bursledon, on the Hamble River, from 1976 to 1979 (between 1987 and 1989 the Profile was resurrected by Maidboats and Paul Hadley Yacht Sales and another 15 were built).

There are two versions of the Profile, one with a two-berth aft cabin and open-backed wheelhouse and one with an aft cockpit and an enclosed wheelhouse, which has a settee you can pull out to form a double berth. In both versions there are four more berths forward — two vee berths up in the bow and a convertible dinette.

The standard engine installation, in the '76 to '79 boats, is a pair of 42hp Mercedes diesels, giving a top speed of about 8½ knots. Good sea boats, they can cruise comfortably at little short of full speed in all but very poor conditions.

A semi-displacement version of the Profile, called the Pursuit 34, has flattened sections aft. Only five were built.

KING FALCON 33

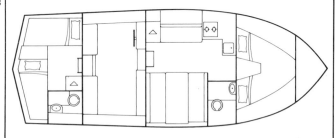

Length overall	33ft 4in (10.16m)
Beam	12ft 2in (3.69m)
Draught	3ft 2in (0.94m)
Hull/deck material	GRP

WILLIAM Osborne of Littlehampton built just a dozen King Falcon 33s, but as one would expect from these leading builders of RNLI lifeboats their motor cruisers earned themselves a reputation as good, seaworthy craft. The first King Falcon was launched in 1972, the last in 1978. Construction of hull, decks and cabin sides is in GRP, but the open-backed wheelhouse and the cabin top is of marine ply.

There's accommodation for six, with two berths in a forward cabin, two in the saloon — from a convertible dinette — and two in an aft cabin, which has its own toilet compartment.

Hull shape is a rather unusual semi-displacement form, round-bilged at midships and ragged-chine aft. Most of the earlier boats have twin 145hp Perkins diesels, with a top speed of 22 to 23 knots, while the later ones have 180hp Ford Mermaids, giving up to 25 knots.

BIRCHWOOD 33/35

	Birchwood 33	Birchwood 35
Length overall	33ft 6in (10.21m)	35ft 0in (10.67m)
Beam	11ft 2in (3.40m)	11ft 2in (3.40)
Draught	2ft 9in (0.91m)	3ft 0in (0.91m)
Hull/deck material	GRP	GRP

FORMERLY known as the Newport 33, then GT33, neither of which were built in great numbers, the Birchwood 33, as Birchwood Boats called it when they took over the moulds, was launched in 1973. They built over 300 up to 1982 and, between 1975 and 1981, 100 of an extended version, the Birchwood 35. The photograph shows a Birchwood 33, the drawings a GT33.

The 33-footer has six berths — four forward and two in an aft cabin. Early boats have a midships, open-backed wheelhouse but in 1981 the boat was restyled to give an enclosed wheelhouse and a flying bridge. The 35 sleeps four in its aft cockpit version, six in the aft cabin version. Some boats have just an inside helm position, some have a second helm on a flying bridge or, on some aft cabin boats, on the raised aft deck.

Graham Caddick designed the hull, which is medium-vee but with rounded underwater sections, and with a deepish keel. Various single and (more common) twin inboard engine installations were fitted. A pair of 150hp diesels would give a top speed of about 20 knots in a 33 and 18 knots in a 35.

129

DS 110

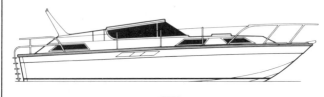

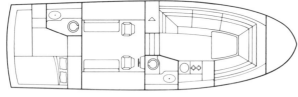

DESIGNED by Don Shead, the DS110 is derived from his highly successful deep-vee offshore powerboats of the mid- to late-1960s. About 40 boats of the class were built by Halmatic between 1968 and 1974.

The vast open cockpit, with seating for up to ten people, looks commonplace in this age of the sports cruiser, but in 1968 it was quite revolutionary. So was the interior accommodation, which includes an aft cabin reached through a hatch in the cockpit seating. There are two berths here and two in the forward cabin, each cabin having its own toilet compartment.

The boats are powered by twin diesels, mostly Ford Sabres of 180hp, which give top speeds of 28 to 30 knots, or 250hp, which push the boat along at up to 35 knots.

Length overall	34ft 0in (10.36m)
Beam	10ft 2in (3.10m)
Draught	3ft 0in (0.91m)
Hull/deck material	GRP

NELSON 34

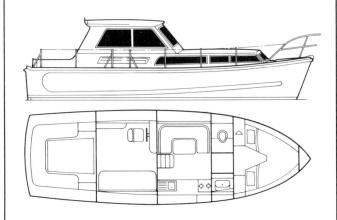

ONE of the famous Nelson range of semi-displacement, round-bilge motorboats designed by TT Boat Designs, Nelson 34s were and still are moulded by Tylers of Tonbridge. Most of the 150-plus boats produced since 1964 have been built as workboats, a couple of dozen as motor yachts. In the early years most 34s were fitted out by Keith, Nelson and other Bembridge yards. Various builders and individuals have fitted them out since the mid-1970s.

The Mk1 version has a fairly basic interior layout with two berths, galley and toilet, and a large cockpit and open-backed wheelhouse. The Mk2 has a larger cabin, with four berths (some Mk2s, incidentally, have wooden decks and/or superstructures). The Mk3 also has four berths, but split between the forward accommodation and an aft cabin.

Various twin diesel installations were fitted — Perkins, Ford Sabre or Ford Thonycroft, up to 2 × 300hp. Top speeds range from about 15 knots to 20 knots, depending on engines. Like the other Nelsons, the 34 has a reputation as an excellent sea boat.

Length overall	34ft 0in (10.36m)
Beam	10ft 0in (3.05m)
Draught	2ft 9in (0.84m)
Hull/deck material	GRP

ROYAL 34

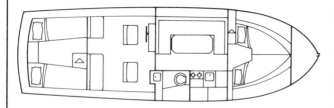

Length overall	34ft 0in (10.36m)
Beam	10ft 6in (3.20m)
Draught	3ft 1in (0.94m)
Hull/deck material	wood or GRP/wood

THE Royal 34, or Royal Cruiser IV as it used to be known, was around from 1963 until 1988, a record lifespan for a production motorboat. About 200 were imported into the UK from Swedish builders Storebro Bruks AB, renowned for the high standard of their construction and finish.

Hull construction was in wood (mahogany on oak) until 1970, wood or GRP from then until 1979 and GRP only thereafter. The GRP boats have wooden (teak on marine ply) decks and with plenty of mahogany trim in the superstructure they still look as though they are all wood. There are two berths in an aft cabin, two in the saloon and two in a forward cabin. Most boats have an open-backed wheelhouse but some have an extended, enclosed wheelhouse. A few have flying bridges. The photograph shows an older, wooden boat and the drawing a later, GRP version.

The hull form is semi-displacement. The first boats were fitted with two 95hp Volvo diesels, giving a top speed of about 12 knots. Later models had increasingly powerful engines, up to twin 192hp Volvos, which gave 25 knots.

WEYMOUTH HALMATIC 34

Length overall	34ft 6in (10.52m)
Beam	11ft 9in (3.59m)
Draught	2ft 10in (0.86m)
Hull/deck material	GRP

THE Weymouth 34 was designed by John Askham for James & Caddy, who built the first one in 1974 based on a hull moulded by Halmatic. When Halmatic took over James & Caddy in 1975 they continued to build (and are still building) this handsome and seaworthy semi-displacement cruiser. About 30 have been built to date. Some have been fitted out by Halmatic themselves — still called Weymouth 34s — and some have been fitted out by other yards and are called either Halmatic 34s or the yards' own names. For instance the F Booker Marine version is called the Humber 35.

Interior layouts vary. The most usual has six berths: two in a forward cabin, two in the main saloon (a convertible dinette) and a pull-out double in the wheelhouse-cum-deck saloon.

Hull form is basically round-bilge, but with almost flat underwater sections aft. Various engine installations have been fitted, all twin diesel. The most common were either 120 or 180hp Ford Sabres, giving about 20 or 22 knots.

BROOM 35 EUROPEAN

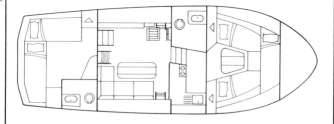

Length overall	34ft 10in (10.62m)
Beam	12ft 2in (3.71m)
Drauht	3ft 0in (0.91m)
Hull/deck material	GRP

DESIGNED by John Bennett and built by the much respected Norfolk boatyard of C J Broom & Sons, the Broom 35 European is a semi-displacement cruiser with a midships wheelhouse/saloon and — a distinctive Broom feature — an outside helm position on a raised aft deck rather than on a flybridge. Broom's built 157 Europeans from 1973 to 1983.

The boat sleeps up to six, with two berths in an aft cabin, two in a forward cabin and a settee that converts into a double berth in the wheelhouse/saloon. Access to this is via sliding doors on either side and a companionway from the aft deck.

The hull is basically medium-vee but with slightly concave underwater sections and a three-quarter length keel. Twin diesel installations of various makes and powers have been fitted. Most of the earlier boats have two 115hp Perkins, which give a top speed of about 16 knots. A few are powered by two 145hp Perkins (20 knots plus) and some by 120hp Ford Mercrafts (15 to 16 knots), while most of the later boats have 140hp Volvos (18 to 19 knots).

BROOM 35 SEDAN

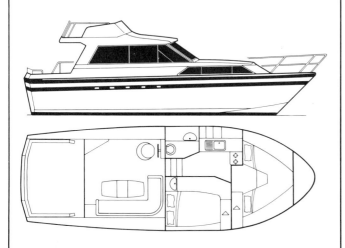

DESIGNER John Bennett based the Broom 35 Sedan on the same medium-vee hull as the Broom 35 European, but gave it a completely different deck and superstructure, to give a boat with an aft cockpit and a flying bridge. C J Broom & Sons built 50 Sedans between 1977 and 1984.

There are six berths, as in the European, but with two forward cabins rather than one forward and one aft, and with a similar convertible settee cum double berth arrangement in the wheelhouse/saloon.

Broom 35 Sedans are powered by a variety of twin-diesel installations. The most common is a pair of 145hp Perkins, which should give a top speed of 20 knots or more.

Length overall	34ft 10in (10.62m)
Beam	12ft 2in (3.71m)
Draught	3ft 0in (0.91m)
Hull/deck material	GRP

PEGASUS 35

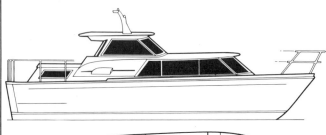

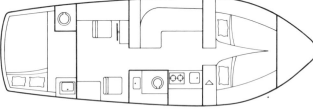

Length overall	34ft 10in (10.62m)
Beam	11ft 2in (3.40m)
Draught	3ft 0in (0.61m)
Hull/deck material	wood or GRP

THE first Pegasus 35, launched at the 1969 London Boat Show, took part in the Round Britain powerboat race later the same year, winning the Best All-rounder, Concours d'Elegance and Index of Performance prizes. Despite this flying start, and the good reputation Pegasus 35s earned for their high standard of construction (hulls in cold-moulded mahogany) and good performance, only 13 boats were built before production ceased in 1973.

Cox & Haswell designed the boat and it was built by Pegasus Marine of Lymington. Except for two boats which were built in GRP, construction was of cold-moulded mahogany with Cascover nylon hull sheathing. Most of the boats were built to the standard layout, giving six berths — two in an aft cabin and four in a spacious, open-plan forward cabin. There is a single helm position in an open-backed wheelhouse.

Early boats were fitted with two 145hp Perkins diesels, giving a top speed of over 25 knots; later ones with upgraded (175hp) versions of the same engines, with which top speed is nearly 30 knots.

TRIANA TANTARELLA

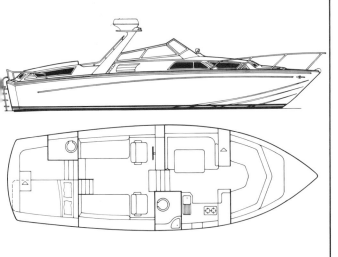

RENATO Levi designed the Tantarella and the boat has the distinctive Levi reverse sheer and, underwater, a genuine deep-vee hull. Levi has been responsible for some of the best fast seagoing boats around and the Tantarella is no exception. It has never been produced in great numbers but builders Triana Boats are still in business, turning out one or two a year. A total of 45 have been built to date.

The boat sleeps six with four berths in the open-plan forward accommodation and two in an aft cabin, with toilet compartments forward and aft. On most boats the helm position is open to the elements in the midships cockpit but a few boats were fitted with hard tops.

Power comes from various twin diesel engine installations, from 145hp Perkins to 300hp Mitsubishis but most commonly Ford Sabres from 180s to 275s. A pair of 250hp Sabres, the most popular option, gives a top speed of over 30 knots.

Length overall 35ft 6in (10.82m)
Beam 11ft 4in (3.45m)
Draught 2ft 10in (0.86m)
Hull/deck material .... GRP

RANGER 36

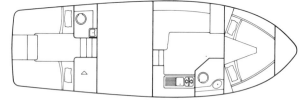

Length overall	35ft 8in (10.87m)
Beam	12ft 3in (3.74m)
Draught	2ft 10in (0.86m)
Hull/deck material	GRP

DELL Quay Sales introduced the Ranger 36, designed by Carey Golesworthy, in 1969. Northshore Yacht Yards took over production in 1971. The last of a total of 25 boats was launched in 1982.

There is sleeping accommodation for six, including two berths in an aft cabin. The forward accommodation comes in one of two versions, one basically open-plan, the other with a separate forward cabin. The midships wheelhouse varies too; on the earliest boats it is open to the stern and with open access to the side decks. Later boats have sliding doors on both sides, to give more protection, and later still the wheelhouses are completely enclosed.

Hull shape is deep-vee. Dell Quay installed twin 175hp Perkins or 180hp Ford Sabres (both diesels), giving top speeds of about 23 or 24 knots, but Northshore introduced a pair of 210hp Sabres as the standard engine, increasing top speed to 25 or 26 knots.

MONACO 36

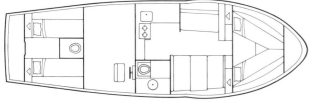

THE Monaco 36 was designed and built by Morgan Giles Ltd of Teignmouth, Devon, and was a development of a 35-footer they had produced in 1958. Between 1959 and 1964 the yard turned out about 30 Monaco 36s, then started building larger motor yachts, of various sizes up to 48ft. Construction was of marine mahogany ply on Canadian rock elm frames, the hull sheathed up to the waterline with GRP.

The standard layout has sleeping accommodation for up to seven — two in an aft cabin, two forward and three in the large deck saloon — with a single, outside helm position.

Hull shape is medium-vee back to midships, shallow-vee aft. Most 36s were fitted with twin Lister diesels of between 80 and 110hp each, the latter driving the boat at up to 16 knots, while a few had 100 or 135hp Perkins diesels. *Monaco Mercury*, a racing powerboat based on a Monaco 36 hull and powered by two 270hp Caterpillar diesels, finished 9th in the 1963 Cowes-Torquay powerboat race.

Length overall	36ft 0in (10.97m)
Beam	11ft 0in (3.35m)
Draught	2ft 4in (0.71m)
Hull/deck material	wood

MORELAND 36

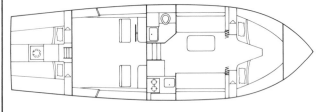

Length overall 36-38ft (11-11.6m)	
Beam 11ft 6in (3.51m)	
Draught 2ft 10in (0.86m)	
Hull/deck material ....wood	

ALTHOUGH only a dozen Morelands were built, these substantial fast cruisers made quite an impact during the 1960s. Several competed in Cowes-Torquay powerboat races and though they were never in contention for overall honours they did twice win the coveted Concours d'Elegance award. One of the Concours winners, *Ja-Conja*, finished eighth overall in the 1966 race. Morelands were built of cold-moulded mahogany, cascover sheathed, by R & W Clark (Cowes), the first in 1961, the last in 1969.

Accommodation varied from boat to boat but they usually had four berths or (those fitted with an aft cabin) six, with an open-backed wheelhouse.

Designed by the builders, the Moreland has a 'warped bottom' hull configuration, deep-vee from bow to midships, medium-vee aft. Earlier boats were fitted with two GM diesels, from 190 to 270hp each (29 knots top speed with 270s), while most of the latter boats are powered by Cummins diesels, of various horsepowers, up to 2 × 300hp, as fitted in *Ja-Conja*.

POWLES 36

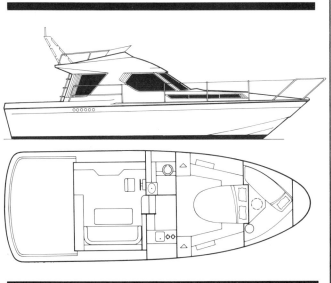

BERNARD Olesinski, who designed most of the current range of Fairlines and Princesses, made his name with several of the range of fast cruisers built by Jack Powles International of Wroxham, including the Powles 36. Between 1975 and 1978, some 45 Powles 36s were built.

The standard version has six berths, with an owner's stateroom and small guest cabin forward and a convertible settee in the wheelhouse/saloon. However, all but a few of the boats have the alternative 'Mediterranean' version which has just four berths — a larger owner's stateroom and no guest cabin. Both have an aft cockpit and a flying bridge.

Hull shape is semi deep-vee — that is, deep-vee forward and midships, medium-vee aft. Most 36s are powered by twin 210 or 212hp Ford Sabre diesels. Top speed should be about 25 knots.

Length overall	36ft 0in (10.97m)
Beam	12ft 3in (3.73m)
Draught	3ft 0in (0.91m)
Hull/deck material	GRP

ROYAL 36

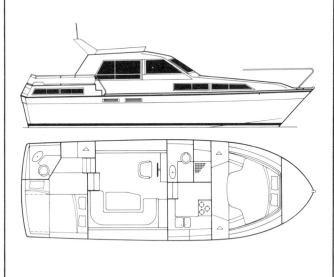

Length overall	36ft 1in (11.00m)
Beam	12ft 7in (3.83m)
Draught	3ft 11in (1.19m)
Hull/deck material	GRP

THE Royal 36, another cruiser from the high-class Swedish yard of Storebro Bruks, was launched in 1982 and was in production until 1988, during which time about 120 were built. Only a dozen were imported into the UK, largely because of delivery problems, demand outstripping supply. The boat has five berths, including three in an aft cabin which has its own toilet compartment. There's a spacious midships saloon-cum-wheelhouse, with a second helm position up on the flying bridge.

With two 220hp Volvo diesels, the early boats had a top speed of about 23 knots. Later boats have 294hp or 350hp versions of the same engine, and top speeds of about 26 and 28 knots respectively. Like all the Royals, the 36 has a reputation as an excellent sea boat and this, combined with the very high standard of construction and fitting out, makes it more expensive than most other cruisers of the same size, but a well-maintained secondhand Royal holds its value well.

DE GROOT 11-METRE

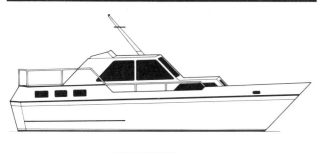

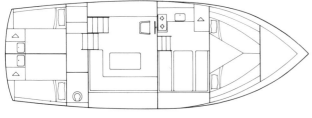

Length overall	36ft 1in (10.99m)
Beam .... 10ft 8in (3.25m) or 12ft 6in (3.81m)
Draught	3ft 0in (0.91m)
Hull/deck material .... steel

THE Dutch firm of de Groot specialises in building steel hulls and superstructures in kit form. In the late 1960s, through the '70s and into the early '80s, their displacement motor cruisers were popular in the UK, a total of 250 being imported during that period by P G Steelcraft. The most successful size was the 11-metre, of which between 40 and 50 kits were imported. Two versions, of different beam, were provided, the narrower generally to be found on rivers and fitted with single engines, the wider favoured for seagoing and powered by twin engines.

Accommodation varies of course, but usually there are eight or nine berths, including two in an aft cabin, with two helm positions, one in the midships wheelhouse/saloon and one on the raised aft deck.

Most owners fitted either a single diesel, usually of between 80 and 100hp, or twin diesels up to 120hp each. With a single engine top speed would be about 9 knots. With twin 120s the boat could break through the displacement speed barrier up to 10 or 11 knots.

MOONRAKER 36

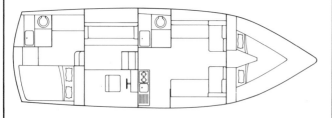

Length overall	36ft 1in (11.00m)
Beam	11ft 6in (3.51m)
Draught	3ft 0in (0.91m)
Hull/deck material	GRP

THE Moonraker 36 was one of the most popular medium-size fast cruisers of the 1970s. The boat was launched in 1970 by Moonraker Marine of Brundall, Norfolk, which later became JCL Marine, and nearly 400 boats were built before JCL went into liquidation in 1980.

The reasons for the boat's popularity were its competitive price (the early examples cost under £10,000 with the smallest engine option of twin 100hp GM diesels) and good accommodation, with a total of six berths — two in an aft cabin, two in the saloon (a convertible dinette) and two in a forward cabin. All but the very early boats had an enclosed wheelhouse and a second helm position on a flybridge.

The hull, designed by Robert Tucker, is deep-vee forward and midships, medium-vee aft. Most Moonrakers were fitted with twin Perkins 145hp or 175hp diesels, giving top speeds of 18 to 20, or 22 to 24 knots, respectively. With the two 100hp GMs top speed, if you are lucky, is 15 knots, which means cruising at 12 or 13.

GRAND BANKS 36

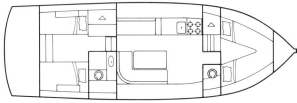

THIS is the boat that launched the term 'trawler yacht' and, specifically, the excellent Grand Banks range. Based on the hard-chine hull form of the Pacific Grand Banks trawlers, the GB36, designed by Ken Smith of the USA, was launched by American Marine in 1963. The first boats were built in Hong Kong, but in 1970 production was transferred to Singapore. Until 1973 construction was in wood (mahogany planking, teak decks). Since then — the boat is still being produced — hull and superstructure have been of GRP. Altogether about 1000 have been built, of which about 120 have been imported into the UK.

The boat sleeps up to six, in forward and aft cabins and in the roomy saloon/wheelhouse. The latter has a settee that can be converted into a double berth, and also houses the galley. Outside, there's plenty of deck space and a large flying bridge.

Most GB36s are fitted with twin Lehmans, of 120hp (pre-1984) or 135hp. Top speed is about 10 knots with 120s, 11 to 12 knots with 135s.

Length overall	36ft 4in (11.07m)
Beam	12ft 2in (3.71m)
Draught	2ft 11in (1.19m)
Hull/deck material	wood or GRP

FAIRLINE 36 TURBO

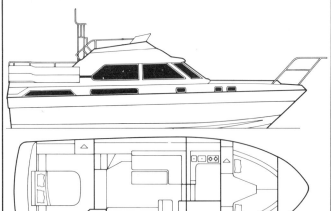

Length overall	36ft 6in (11.13m)
Beam	13ft 4in (4.06m)
Draught	3ft 4in (1.01m)
Hull/deck material	GRP

DESIGNED by Bernard Olesinski, the Fairline 36 Turbo was launched in 1981 and is still in production. Fairline Boats of Oundle, Northamptonshire have built about 250.

The 36 Turbo has berths for six to eight people, with a double in the large 'owner's stateroom' aft cabin, two singles in the forward cabin and settees and/or dinettes that can provide another two, three or four berths in the wheelhouse/saloon, depending on which of several layout variations the boat has (the 36 Sedan, based on the same hull but without the aft cabin, was introduced in 1986).

Hull shape is deep-vee from the entry back to midships, levelling out to medium-vee at the transom, and has broad chine flats. Twin Volvo inboard diesels of between 150hp and 300hp (each) give maximum speeds of between 21 and 30 knots.

HAGG 36

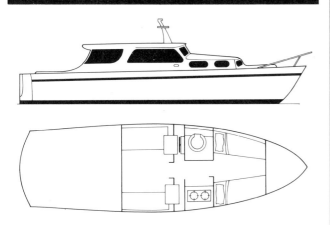

Length overall	36ft 6in (11.13m)
Beam	11ft 0in (3.35m)
Draught	2ft 6in (0.76m)
Hull/deck material	wood or GRP/wood

WITH its streamlined, low-profile superstructure, the Hagg 36, designed by the late Arthur Hagg, is one of the most distinctive production motor cruisers ever built.

Between 1962 and 1970 the Dorset Yacht Company of Poole built 35 Hagg 36s. Early boats were built entirely in marine ply, but those launched from 1964 onwards have GRP hulls and, except for a few that were all GRP, marine ply decks and superstructures. The photograph is of one of the earlier wooden boats, the drawings of a later GRP version; note the change of deck line.

There's sleeping accommodation for four, with two berths in a forecabin and two more in the wheelhouse/saloon. Aft of this there's a loggia, an open area partly covered by an extension of the wheelhouse top, and aft of that an open cockpit (on some later boats the loggia is fully enclosed).

Hagg 36s are powered by a variety of engines, most commonly a pair of 145hp Perkins diesels, giving top speeds of 22 to 24 knots. Some of the earlier, petrol-powered boats have been re-engined with diesels. With their semi-displacement, round-bilge hull form, the boats have a reputation for soft riding and seaworthiness.

OTTER 36/40

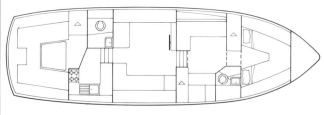

THE handsome Otter class displacement motor yachts were designed by J Francis Jones & Partners. The Otter 36 and 40 were similar in appearance and layout, the 40 being just a little more spacious and, reputedly, the better sea boat. Otters were built by various yards, between 1966 and 1971, sadly in no great numbers — nine or ten 36s and only three 40s. E C Landamore & Co and Porter & Haylett, both of Wroxham, were the most prolific, building eight Otters between them. Construction is of mahogany or iroko planking on oak frames.

An unusual feature of the standard interior layout is the positioning of the main saloon and galley aft in the spacious area under the raised aft deck. Layouts vary in detail but the boats can have as many as seven berths. There are two helm positions, one in the wheelhouse and one on the aft deck.

Various twin diesel installations can be found in Otters, including 60hp Thornycrofts and 72hp Perkins. Top speed of a 36 would be little more than 8 knots, of a 40 about 9.

The illustrations are of a Landamore-built Otter 40.

	Otter 36	Otter 40
Length overall	36ft 6in (11.13m)	40ft 0in (12.19m)
Beam	11ft 6in (3.51m)	12ft 4in (3.76m)
Draught	3ft 2in (0.97m)	3ft 6in (1.07m)
Hull/deck material	wood	wood

OCEAN PIRATE

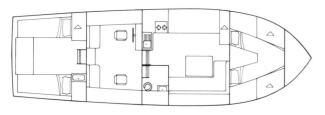

DESIGNED and built by Brooke Marine, of Lowestoft, Suffolk, specialists in aluminium construction, the Ocean Pirate was launched in 1965. Until 1968 the boats were 36ft 8in long but the design was then extended to 40ft. Altogether 21 were built, the last 40-footer in 1976. Most of the 40-footers were built as police boats but some as express cruisers, including the first one, called *Ocean Pirate*, which took part in the 1969 Round Britain Powerboat Race, finishing seventh overall.

Ocean Pirates were virtually custom built as far as the layout was concerned but most have six berths, including two in an aft cabin. The one helm position has a wheelshelter.

Brooke Marine called the hull shape of the Ocean Pirate 'geoform'; it utilises a variation of the 'warped bottom' configuration with deep-vee sections forward and midships, flattening towards the stern. Power comes from twin Perkins or Cummins diesels, usually of 135-280hp, with top speeds of up to 25 knots.

Illustrated is a 36ft 8in Ocean Pirate.

	pre 1968	post 1968
Length overall	36ft 8in (11.18m)	40ft 0in (12.19m)
Beam	11ft 10in (3.61m)	11ft 10in (3.61m)
Draught	3ft 4in (0.99m)	3ft 6in (1.07m)
Hull/deck material	aluminium	aluminium

BIRCHWOOD 37

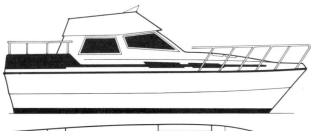

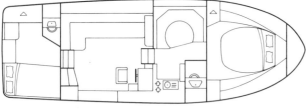

Length overall	37ft 0in (11.28m)
Beam	12ft 4in (3.76m)
Draught	3ft 6in (1.07m)
Hull/deck material	GRP

LAUNCHED in 1981, the Birchwood 37 President was in production until 1984, by which time Birchwood Boat Co had built about 60 boats. It was superseded by the Birchwood TS37, which is still in production.

There's accommodation for six, with double berths in forward and aft cabins and a dinette convertible into another double, and there are two helm positions, one in the wheelhouse/saloon and one on a flying bridge.

The boat has the familiar Birchwood hull shape with rounded sections in the bow but medium-vee from midships aft, and a three-quarter-length keel. Power is provided by twin diesels of various makes and powers. A pair of 215hp Ford Mermaids gives a top speed of about 24 knots.

BROOM 37

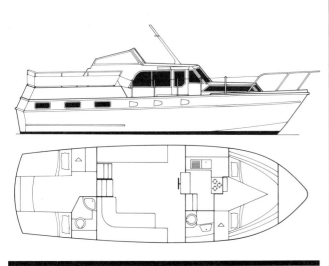

THE Broom 37 Continental was launched in 1968 and was succeeded in 1978 by the Broom 37 Crown, basically the same boat but with restyled superstructure and interior, which remained in production up to 1986. The boat was designed by John Bennett, moulded by Aqua-Fibre and fitted out to high standards by C J Broom & Sons of Brundall, Norfolk (who took over Aqua-Fibre in 1970). Broom's produced 186 Continentals and 83 Crowns. Illustrated is the Broom 37 Continental.

There is accommodation for six, with two berths in a spacious aft cabin (singles in the Continental, a double in the Crown), two in a forward cabin and a pull-out settee in the wheelhouse/saloon. Both models have a second helm position outside on the aft deck. The wheelhouse/saloon has sliding side doors and access to the aft deck.

The semi-displacement hull has slightly concave underwater sections, flattening towards the stern, with a three-quarter-length keel. Continentals are generally powered by two 145hp Perkins diesels (top speed 17 to 18 knots), Crowns by two 150hp Volvo diesels (18 to 19 knots).

Length overall	37ft 0in (11.28m)
Beam	12ft 4in (3.76m)
Draught	3ft 0in (0.91m)
Hull/deck material	GRP

OCEAN 37

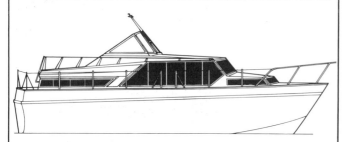

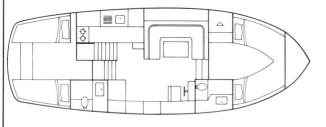

Length overall 37ft 0in (11.28m)
Beam 12ft 0in (3.66m)
Draught 3ft 0in (0.91m)
Hull/deck material .... GRP

BASED on the same hull as the Broom 37, the Ocean 37 was Aqua-Fibre's own version of the boat. Aqua-Fibre built 157 Ocean 37s between 1973 and 1983.

The accommodation layout is almost identical to that on the Broom 37, with six berths in forward and aft cabins and in the wheelhouse/saloon. The boat has an outside helm position over the aft cabin, as on the Broom, though the cabin is not in this case full-width. And unlike the Broom, the Ocean has no side doors into the wheelhouse/saloon.

Most Ocean 37s are powered by twin 145hp Perkins diesels, giving a top speed of 17 to 18 knots. A few boats, mostly exported ones, have twin 175hp Perkins, pushing the top speed up to about 19 knots.

PRINCESS 37

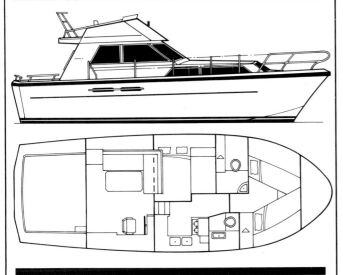

MARINE Projects built over 350 Princess 37s, from 1973 to 1981. She was one of the many Princesses designed by John Bennett.

The boat sleeps six in three separate cabins, including the wheelhouse/saloon, which has a dinette-cum-double berth, and there are two toilet/shower compartments.

Like the Princess 33, the boat was unusual in being available with a choice of hulls — Y-shaped or deep-vee, the former with flattish aft sections and a long shallow keel, designed for displacement and semi-displacement speeds, the latter designed for high speed.

The Y-hull boats were most commonly fitted with two 120hp Ford Mermaid inboard diesels, driving the boat at up to 16 or 17 knots. The deep-vee models were fitted with a variety of twin inboard diesels. A pair of 180hp Ford Mermaids, giving a top speed of 18 to 20 knots, was the most popular option on the earlier boats. Many later ones have more powerful engines, such as 235hp Volvo TAMD60s, which should drive the boat at up to 22 knots.

Length overall	37ft 1in (11.30m)
Beam	13ft 0in (3.96m)
Draught	3ft 0in (0.91m)
Hull/deck material	GRP

MAMBA 37

THE late Colin Chapman of Lotus Cars and JCL Marine designed the Mamba as an express cruiser, with a deep-vee hull and a superstructure that owed much to Italian thinking in how such a boat should look. Between 1976 and 1981, when they went into liquidation, JCL Marine of Brundall, Norfolk, built 14 Mambas.

The accent is on style rather than plentiful sleeping accommodation, with just two permanent berths — a double in the forward cabin. A settee in the wheelhouse/saloon can be converted into a single or double berth. However, there is plenty of room to move around, both inside and up on the flying bridge, which is extended aft to overhang the cockpit.

The boats are powered by twin 180hp Ford Mercraft diesels, working through V-drives and giving a top speed of about 30 knots.

Length overall	37ft 6in (11.43m)
Beam	11ft 10in (3.61m)
Draught	3ft 8in (1.12m)
Hull/deck material	GRP

FAIRWAYS TRAWLER 38

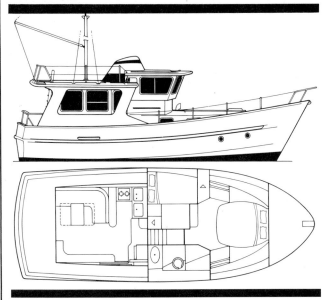

A distinctive trawler yacht, with its broad, 'lantern' wheelhouse, the Fairways Trawler 38 was designed by Wyatt and Freeman and built by Fairways Marine, who produced about 40 of the boats between 1978 and 1981, when they went into liquidation.

The boat has four permanent berths, in two forward cabins, and on some models the settee in the deck saloon can be converted into a double berth. The exterior layout has some striking features: the high bulwarks (especially in the bow where they give the deck line an accentuated sheer); the sheltered side decks; and the mini flying bridge inside a false funnel on the coachroof.

Underwater hull shape is round bilge with a keel, with flat enough sections aft to enable semi-displacement performance. Power comes from twin Ford Sabre diesels of between 120 and 300hp each. Top speed with twin 120s is 12 to 13 knots, with the commonly fitted 212hp Sabres, 17 to 18 knots.

Length overall	37ft 9in (11.51m)
Beam	13ft 9in (4.19m)
Draught	3ft 9in (1.14m)
Hull/deck material	GRP

AQUA-STAR 38

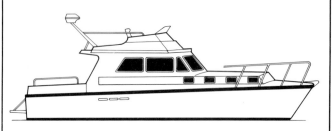

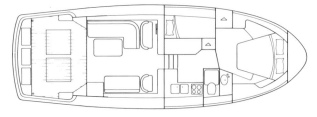

Length overall	38ft 0in (11.58m)
Beam	12ft 9in (3.89m)
Draught	3ft 6in (1.07m)
Hull/deck material	GRP

LIKE the 27, 32 and 33, the Aqua-Star 38, launched in 1978, has been built in various pleasure as well as commercial versions, to cater for those who want a pure cruising boat and for those who want something that is also suitable for fishing or diving. Aqua-Star Ltd of Guernsey have built about 75 non-commercial versions of the 38 to date.

The deck and interior layout can vary considerably even within the basic three types. These are: Fast Sports Fisherman, which has a large aft cockpit and berths for four to six in the forward cabin and wheelhouse; Oceanranger aft cockpit (illustrated), which has six berths in three separate cabins, including the wheelhouse-cum-deck saloon; and Oceanranger aft cabin, which has eight or nine berths with a midships wheelhouse/saloon and an outside, aft-deck helm position, and which was introduced in 1983.

The 38 has a round-bilge, semi-displacement hull. Various twin diesels, from 2 × 105 to 2 × 250hp, have been fitted. A pair of 180s in an Oceanranger should give a top speed of about 20 knots.

COLVIC TRAWLER 38

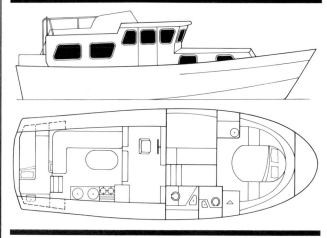

Length overall	38ft 0in (11.58m)
Beam	13ft 0in (3.96m)
Draught	3ft 6in (1.07m)
Hull/deck material	GRP

JOHN Bennett designed the Colvic Trawler 38 for Colvic Craft, who produce the hull and deck mouldings for boatyard or private completion. Colvic introduced this fast trawler yacht in 1977 and built just under 100, up to 1988. The best known version of the boat is the **Beta 40**, from Jarman's Boatyard.

Apart from the basic concept of a large, split-level deck saloon and wheelhouse, the interior layout varies considerably. There are four variations even in the Beta 40, two versions of which have a small aft cabin with two berths and six further berths split between two forward cabins and the saloon. On some boats, including the Beta 40, part of the large expanse of superstructure top — stretching over the full width of the boat to shelter the side decks — is used as a flying bridge.

A pair of 180hp Ford Sabres has been one of the most popular engine options, for a top speed of 18 to 19 knots.

POWLES 36+2 and SUPER 38

AS the name suggests, the Powles 36+2 is a stretched (by 2ft) version of the Powles 36. The Powles Super 38 is based on the same hull as the 36+2 and has a very similar layout, but its superstructure is noticeably more streamlined.

Bernard Olesinski was the designer, Jack Powles International the builder. Between 1977 and 1981, eighteen Powles 36+2s were built. The Super 38, of which thirty were built, was in production from 1980 to 1982. The photographs and drawings show a Super 38.

Both boats have an aft cockpit and accommodation for up to six people, with four permanent berths in two cabins forward and a convertible settee in the wheelhouse/saloon. Both have a flying bridge and aft cockpit, but on the 38 the flying bridge is extended aft, providing more room up top and some shelter in the cockpit.

Hull form is 'semi deep-vee' (deep-vee at midships, medium-vee aft). The 36+2s are usually fitted with twin 212hp Ford Sabre diesels, the 38s with twin 220hp Volvo diesels or the 212hp Sabres. Top speeds are in the region of 23 to 25 knots.

Length overall	38ft 0in (11.58m)
Beam	12ft 3in (3.73m)
Draught	3ft 0in (0.91m)
Hull/deck material	GRP

POWLES 38

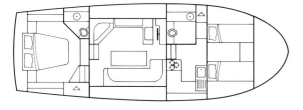

Length overall	38ft 0in (11.58m)
Beam	13ft 2in (4.01m)
Draught	3ft 0in (0.91m)
Hull/deck material	GRP

THE Powles 38 was the first of several fast cruisers from Jack Powles International to be designed by Bernard Olesinski, nowadays better known for his boats in the current Fairline and Princess ranges. The boat was launched at the 1973 London Boat Show and 40 were built between then and 1979.

All but one of the boats have an aft cabin, with a total of six berths — two more in the forward cabin and a settee-cum-double berth in the saloon/wheelhouse. Outside, there's a generous amount of deck space, with wide side decks and a spacious raised aft deck (on the aft-cabin boats) from which steps lead up to a flying bridge.

Hull form is medium-vee with a long shallow keel. All the boats are powered by twin diesels, most commonly 235hp Volvos and 175hp Perkins, giving top speeds of about 24 and 20 knots respectively.

PRINCESS 38

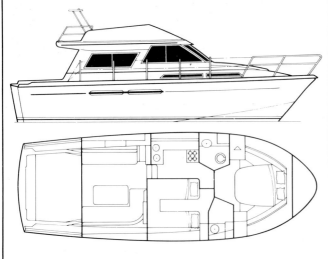

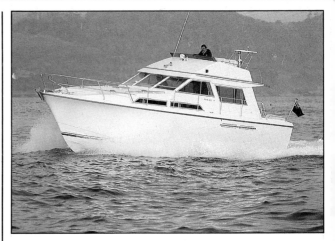

Length overall	38ft 1in (11.61m)
Beam	13ft 0in (3.96m)
Draught	3ft 0in (0.91m)
Hull/deck material	GRP

A SUCCESSOR to the Princess 37, this boat was in production from 1981 to 1985, when it in turn was superseded by the Princess 385. Marine Projects built nearly 200 Princess 38s during that period.

Based on the deep-vee hull version of the 37, but with a redesigned superstructure, the boat has a larger deck saloon-cum-wheelhouse and a larger flying bridge. It also has seven berths rather than six, with four down below in two separate cabins and three in the saloon/wheelhouse.

The most common engine installations are a pair of 188hp Ford Mermaid Majestic diesels, which should drive the boat at up to 21 or 22 knots, and two 235hp Volvo diesels, giving a top speed of 24 to 25 knots.

CLEOPATRA 3750/38

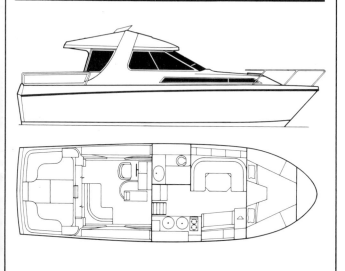

LIKE its smaller sister the Cleopatra 1000 or 33, the 3750 changed its name during its production run, to the Cleopatra 38. The boat is a development of the 33, designed by Pelle Petersen and built by Eastwood Marine at Wallasea Island, Essex, and their successors, Cleopatra Cruisers. It was launched in 1971 and remained in production until 1988. Twenty boats were built.

The accommodation is similar to the 33 with an unusual twin double-berth cabin under the wheelhouse, a convertible dinette in the saloon and a forward cabin, enabling up to eight people to sleep on board, albeit in something of a squash. But there the similarity ends, for all the 3750/38s have an enclosed wheelhouse and a flying bridge.

Engine installation is rather unusual too — a pair of diesels, usually 180hp Ford Sabres or 235hp Volvos, working through V-drives. Top speed is about 20 knots with the Sabres, 22 to 23 knots with the Volvos. Cleopatra Cruisers installed 200hp Volvo outdrive diesels with Duoprops and claimed to be getting 30 knots out of the boats.

Length overall	38ft 5in (11.71m)
Beam	12ft 3in (3.73m)
Draught	3ft 2in (0.97m)
Hull/deck material	GRP

RAMPART 38/39

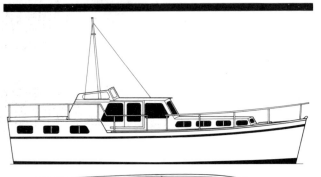

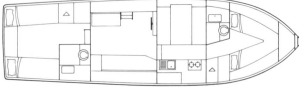

	Rampart 38	Rampart 39
Length overall	38ft 6in (11.73m)	39ft 0in (11.89m)
Beam	10ft 6in (3.20m)	11ft 0in (3.35m)
Draught	3ft 4in (1.01m)	3ft 6in (1.07m)
Hull/deck material	wood	wood

BETWEEN 1970 and 1982 the Southampton firm of Rampart Boatbuilding Co, one of the last outposts of traditional timber construction at least as far as motor cruisers were concerned, built 20 Rampart 38s and 39s. The 39 was a development of the 38.

These heavy-displacement, round-bilge boats were constructed of iroko planking on Canadian rock elm (in later boats danta) frames.

The boats sleep five — two in a forward cabin, one in the wheelhouse/saloon and two in an aft cabin (which is much larger on the 39, being under a full-width raised aft deck). Most 38s and 39s have an additional, outside helm position on the aft deck.

The most common engine installation was a pair of 72hp Perkins diesels, giving a top speed of about 10½ knots.

The illustrations show the Rampart 39.

ROYAL 40

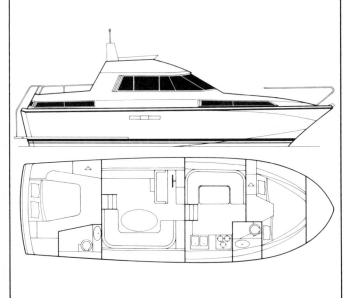

IN production from 1980 to 1987, the Royal 40 was another luxurious cruiser from Storebro Bruks of Sweden, who have now replaced the boat with a new 40-footer, the Royal 400. A dozen 40s were imported into the UK.

A number of interior options were offered, but all have six berths. The Baltic version, as illustrated, has a two-berth aft cabin, the 40 Biscay an aft cockpit, with a dinette in the wheelhouse-cum-saloon which can be converted into a double. Both versions have two berths in the forecabin and two more either from another dinette, opposite the galley, or in another, side cabin. Most boats, of both versions, have two helm positions (wheelhouse and flying bridge).

Like all the other Royals, the 40 has a semi-displacement hull form. Power is provided by two 225hp or 270hp Volvos, giving top speeds of about 18 or 21 knots respectively.

Length overall	39ft 8in (12.09m)
Beam	12ft 10in (3.91m)
Draught	3ft 11in (1.19m)
Hull/deck material	GRP

BATES STAR CRAFT

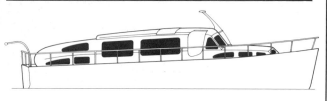

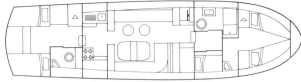

	Star Craft 40	Star Craft 45
Length overall	40ft 0in (12.19m)	45ft 0in (13.72m)
Beam	11ft 5in (3.48m)	11ft 6in (3.51m)
Draught	3ft 6in (1.07m)	3ft 6in (1.07m)
Hull/deck material	wood	wood

W BATES & Son of Chertsey introduced the Bates Star Craft 40 in 1961, followed a year later by the Star Craft 45, virtually identical except in length. Both boats were a development of smaller cruisers bearing the Star Craft name that Bates had been building since the early 1950s. The yard turned out 23 40s and seven 45s, up to 1970. Construction is of double-diagonal planked teak on oak frames.

Star Craft cruisers have a distinctive superstructure, long and low, with an inside helm position forward of amidships. Some boats have an outside helm position also, on the decking over the aft cabin. Interior layouts vary, offering between seven and ten berths.

Round-bilge hulls have flattish sections aft to give enough lift for semi-displacement performance. Most Star Craft have twin Perkins diesels, 105hp each in the earlier models and 145hp in later ones, giving top speeds of about 14 and up to 20 knots respectively.

Illustrations are of a Star Craft 45.

SEALION 40/41

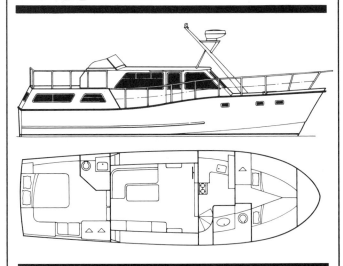

BASED on a 40ft Thornycroft hull with modifications and a new deck and superstructure design by John Bennett, the Sealion 40 was launched by J G Meakes of Marlow in 1967. They built nine of these round-bilge, semi-displacement boats up to 1971 when Tough Bros of Teddington took over the moulds. Over the next five years Tough's built six more boats, but only used the hull mould, building the deck and superstructure in teak, which accounts for the minor increase in length and change of name.

Interior layouts vary but generally include six berths — two in a forward cabin, two in an aft cabin and two in the deck saloon-cum-wheelhouse. All the boats have a second helm position on the aft deck.

Most 40s and 41s are powered by twin 145hp Perkins diesels, giving a top speed of 15 to 16 knots. The later 41s were fitted with the uprated (175hp) versions of the same engine, pushing top speed up to 18 knots.

The photograph shows a Sealion 40, the drawings a 41.

	Sealion 40	Sealion 41
Length overall	40ft 0in (12.12m)	41ft 0in (12.49m)
Beam	12ft 6in (3.81m)	12ft 6in (3.81m)
Draught	3ft 9in (1.14m)	4ft 0in (1.22m)
Hull/deck material	GRP	GRP/Wood

FREEMAN 41

Length overall	41ft 0in (12.50m)
Beam	14ft 0in (4.27m)
Draught	3ft 0in (0.91m)
Hull/deck material	GRP

THE Freeman 41 was the flagship of the Freeman fleet from its introduction in 1977 until its builders, John Freeman (Marine), finished boatbuilding in 1984. By then about fifty 41s had been produced. As in all the other boats in the range, the standard of GRP moulding and interior joinery — in a well-maintained boat — is very high.

The boat sleeps six in three separate cabins, two forward and one aft. There's a large deck saloon-cum-wheelhouse and a flying bridge.

Hull form is medium-vee with a three-quarter-length keel. Power comes from two 212hp Ford Sabre diesels, which should give a top speed of over 20 knots.

NELSON 40/42

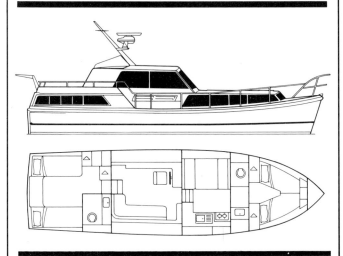

Length overall	41ft 0in (12.50m)
Beam	11ft 9in (3.58m)
Draught	3ft 6in (1.07m)
Hull/deck material	GRP or GRP/wood

NEARLY 300 motor yachts and workboats have been built on the Nelson 40 hull, one of the Nelson range of semi-displacement boats designed by TT Boat Designs and renowned for good seakeeping. Introduced in 1965, the 40 hull is still in production, moulded by Halmatic, of Havant, Hampshire. Until 1970 most were fitted out by Keith Nelson in Bembridge, Isle of Wight. Then other yards took over, giving them their own names, including the **Weymouth 42** (James & Caddy). When Halmatic took over J & C they continued to use the Weymouth name for the boats they fitted out themselves. Other names that crop up include **Humber 42** (boats fitted out by F Booker Marine), **Mallard 42** (T J Clune) and **Channels Islands 42** (Guernsey Boatbuilders).

Until 1968, the deck and superstructure were both wood; from then until 1970 just the superstructure was wood. Since then most boats have been entirely GRP. Various layouts provide berths for five to seven, including two in an aft cabin and, usually, one in the midships wheelhouse.

The boats are powered by twin diesels, most commonly 2 x 180hp or 2 x 250hp Ford Sabres, giving top speeds of about 20 and 25 knots respectively.

PRINCESS 41/412/ 414

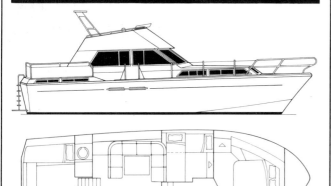

Length overall	41ft 2in (12.55m)
Beam	13ft 0in (3.96m)
Draught	3ft 3in (0.99m)
Hull/deck material	GRP

MARINE Projects of Plymouth built the Princess 41, a stretched version of the Princess 37, from 1977 to 1982, when the boat was superseded by the 414, based on the deep-vee version of the 37 hull but with a modified superstructure and interior layout. The 414s continued in production until 1987. The Princess 412, introduced in 1979, was an aft cockpit version of the same boat. Altogether more than 250 examples of the 41, 412 and 414 were built. The drawings are of a 41, the photograph a 412.

The standard layout on both the 41 and the 414 has eight berths in four separate cabins, including two in an aft cabin and two from a convertible dinette in the wheelhouse/saloon. In the 414 the builders offered the option of a three-sided dinette (convertible to a double berth) opposite the galley in place of one of the cabins. The 412 had seven berths — three in the wheelhouse saloon and four in two cabins down below.

With the standard engine installation of twin 235hp Volvo diesels, top speed is about 24 knots.

TRADER 41 and 41+2

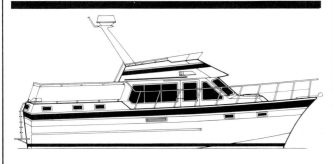

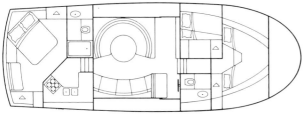

Length overall	41ft 2in (12.55m)
Beam	14ft 10in (4.52m)
Draught	4ft 1in (1.24m)
Hull/deck material	GRP

THE Trader 41 and 41+2 (the same boat only with two more berths) were designed and developed by Tarquin Boat Co of Ringwood, Hampshire, but were — and still are — built in Taiwan. They were introduced in 1980 and 1981 respectively. To date Tarquin have sold 140 boats, of which about 30 (mostly 41+2s) have remained in the UK.

The 41 has four berths in two large cabins, one forward and one aft, and two 'occasional' berths in the wheelhouse/saloon. The 41+2 has two smaller forward cabins, giving an extra two berths. The full-width aft cabin on both boats provides a spacious sundeck above.

Hull shape is medium-vee with a keel, effectively a semi-displacement form. The most popular engine installation has been a pair of 120hp Ford diesels, which drive the boat at up to 12 knots, but more powerful engines have been fitted, up to twin 255hp Caterpillar diesels, pushing top speed up to 22 knots.

FAIRLINE 40

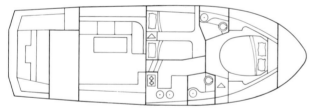

Length overall	41ft 4in (12.60m)
Beam	13ft 2in (4.01m)
Draught	3ft 0in (0.91m)
Hull/deck material	GRP

FAIRLINE Boats introduced what was then the largest of their extensive range of cruisers in 1977, and built 180 until they ceased production in 1988.

There's accommodation for either six or eight, depending on whether the boat has what is a vast stern locker or the tiny two-berth aft cabin that was an extra in the early days but later became standard. The forward cabin, with a large double bed, is the 'owner's stateroom' and there are two single berths, or on some boats a double, in the guest cabin. The settee in the wheelhouse/saloon can be converted into another double.

John Bennett designed the Fairline 40, giving it a medium-vee hull with a shallow, three-quarter length keel. Most 40s were fitted with a pair of 190hp Volvo diesels, top speed being about 22 knots.

C-KIP 40

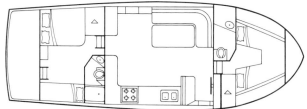

Length overall	41ft 9in (12.73m)
Beam	13ft 8in (4.16m)
Draught	4ft 0in (1.22m)
Hull/deck material	GRP

THE C-Kip 40 was the most popular in a range of Taiwanese-built displacement trawler yachts, from 28ft up to 65ft (8.5m to 20m), imported in the late '70s and early '80s by Kip Marina, on the Firth of Clyde. About 30 C-Kip 40s came into the UK between 1977 and 1982.

There are three versions. The 40 Tri-Cabin has an aft cabin, with a double and a single berth, that can be turned into two cabins with a folding partition. There are two berths in a forward cabin and in the wheelhouse-cum-deck saloon a settee can be converted into a double berth. The 40 Aft Cabin has a broadly similar layout but with a larger, non-dividable double cabin aft. The 40 Sedan has an extended deck saloon, in which up to three could sleep, and two double cabins forward. The photograph shows a 40 Sedan; the drawings are of the 40 Tri-Cabin.

A pair of 120hp Ford Lehman diesels drives the boat at up to 10 or 11 knots.

POWLES 41

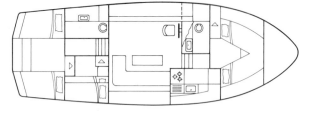

Length overall	41ft 10in (12.75m)
Beam	14ft 6in (4.42m)
Draught	3ft 4in (1.01m)
Hull/deck material	GRP

JACK Powles International of Wroxham, Norfolk, built 47 Powles 41s between 1972 and 1976, and one more in 1980. John Bennett designed this beamy fast cruiser.

The boat sleeps eight, with one cabin forward and two aft, and a settee which pulls out into a double berth in the saloon/wheelhouse. The exterior layout is notable for the fact that the foredeck, wide side decks and large, uncluttered aft deck are all on the same level. The flying bridge is just four steps up from the aft deck.

Hull shape is medium-vee. Twin 145hp Perkins or 235hp Volvo diesels are the most common engine installations, giving maximum speeds of about 24 or 27 knots respectively.

BIRCHWOOD 42 EMPRESS

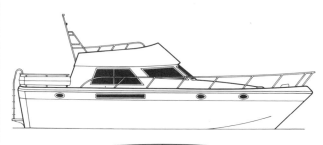

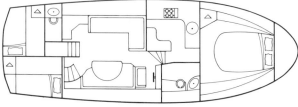

Length overall	42ft 0in (12.80m)
Beam	14ft 3in (4.34m)
Draught	3ft 9in (1.14m)
Hull/deck material	GRP

BASED on the hull of the John Bennett-designed Powles 41 but with Birchwood Boat International's own superstructure and interior layout, the Birchwood 42 Empress was launched in 1982. A dozen boats were built during a three-year production period.

A variety of interior layouts offer berths for six or eight. All versions have a very large wheelhouse-cum-deck saloon and all have a second helm position on a flying bridge.

Hull shape is medium-vee. Power comes from one of several twin Volvo diesel inboard installations, up to 2 × 305hp. A pair of 220s should give a top speed of 20 knots.

KEMROCK ISLE

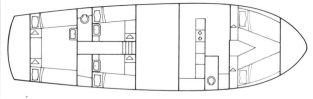

Length overall.................................... 42ft 0in (12.80m)
Beam.. 12ft 0in (3.66m)
Draught.. 3ft 9in (1.14m)
Hull/deck material .... wood

THE Kemrock Isle, a heavy-displacement, round-bilged motor yacht, was designed and marketed by Kemrock Yachts. It was built in Scotland by J & G Forbes of Fraserburgh, of traditional timber construction, using larch planking on oak frames. About 20 were built between 1961 and 1965.

There is accommodation for seven, with one double and two single cabins aft, and a double cabin forward of the large saloon. The helm position is on deck, out in the open except on one or two boats which had open-backed wheelhouses fitted (rather spoiling their appearance).

Power comes from various twin-diesel installations, usually Ford or BMC engines of between 50 and 60hp. Top speed should be between 10-12 knots.

OCEAN 42

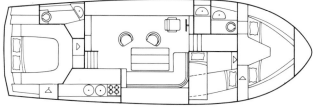

C J BROOM and Sons, of Brundall, Norfolk, built 36 Ocean 42s between 1978 and 1989. This comfortable motor yacht was designed by John Bennett.

Interior layout varies in detail from boat to boat, within the basic format of six berths spread between a large aft cabin and two forward cabins, and with a roomy deck saloon-cum-wheelhouse. There's an outside helm position on the raised aft deck, and on some boats the owners have chosen not to bother with the inside helm position.

The semi-displacement hull is similar to the Ocean and Broom 37s and the Broom 35, with slightly concave underwater sections, flattening towards the stern, and a three-quarter-length keel. Power comes from twin Volvo diesels of between 200 and 300hp, and top speeds range from about 19 to 22 knots.

Length overall	42ft 1in (12.83m)
Beam	14ft 0in (4.27m)
Draught	3ft 3in (0.99m)
Hull/deck material	GRP

MOODY LANCER

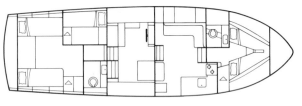

Length overall	42ft 6in (12.95m)
Beam	12ft 8in (3.86m)
Draught	3ft 8in (1.12m)
Hull/deck material	GRP

MOULDED by the Tyler Boat Company and fitted out by A H Moody & Son of Swanwick at the head of the Hamble River, half a dozen Lancers were built between 1968 and 1974. This substantial, round-bilge displacement motor yacht was designed by Graham Moody.

With minor variations in the interior layout, the boats have accommodation for between six and eight. There are two cabins, a second toilet compartment under the large aft deck, a midships wheelhouse, a saloon, fitted with a convertible dinette in some boats, and a two-berth forward cabin. There is a second, outside helm on the aft deck.

All six boats were fitted with a pair of 95hp Perkins diesels, giving a top speed of about 10½ knots.

GRAND BANKS 42

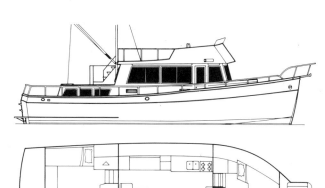

SINCE it was introduced in 1965, the Grand Banks 42 has proved to be the most popular of American Marine's excellent range of luxury trawler yachts. Over 1200 have been built to date, of which about 200 have been imported into the UK. In 1969 production switched from Hong Kong to Singapore, and in 1973 construction switched from wood (mahogany planking, teak decks) to GRP.

The standard layout has two berths in a forward cabin, two in an aft cabin and two in the form of a pull-out settee in the very large saloon/wheelhouse, which also houses the galley. In the 'Europa' layout there's no aft cabin but a large aft deck, the saloon/wheelhouse is further aft and there's a second forward cabin.

Standard engines are a pair of 120hp (pre-1984) or 135hp Ford Lehmans, with which top speed is 11 to 12 knots. But the hard-chine hull form, though basically intended for displacement performance, is suitable for planing and many boats built since the mid-1970s have more powerful engines. A pair of 210hp Caterpillars gives a top speed of 14 knots, 320s 17 knots and 375s 22 knots.

Length overall	42ft 7in (12.98m)
Beam	13ft 7in (4.14m)
Draught	4ft 2in (1.27m)
Hull/deck material	wood or GRP

TREMLETT 42

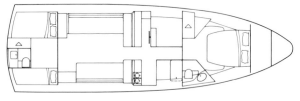

Length overall	42ft 8in (13.01m)
Beam	12ft 0in (3.66m)
Draught	3ft 2in (0.97m)
Hull/deck material	GRP

TREMLETT Boat Sales of Topsham, Devon, launched the Tremlett 42 Offshore in 1977, a development of the 40ft hot-moulded timber boat of which the company had built half a dozen during the previous four years. The 42 is still available today, 63 having been built to date. The boat was designed by Chris Tremlett whose deep-vee hulls have a reputation for excellent seakeeping at high speeds.

Interior layout varies considerably. With an aft cabin there are berths for between six and eight; with an aft cockpit sleeping capacity is four to six. In both cases there are usually two forward cabins and an occasional berth in the wheelhouse/saloon. The photograph is of an aft-cockpit boat, the drawings of the aft-cabin version.

Early 42s were generally fitted with twin 210hp Ford Sabre diesels, giving a top speed of about 28 knots. Later, a pair of 235hp Volvo diesels became the standard, pushing speeds up to about 30 knots. Other installations include 210hp Caterpillars and 335hp Cummins driving through water jets.

MYSTERE & MIRAGE

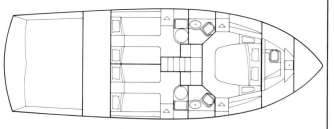

Length overall	43ft 0in (13.11m)
Beam	14ft 4in (4.37m)
Draught	3ft 6in (1.97m)
Hull/deck material	GRP

THE Mystere was built by JCL Marine of Brundall, Norfolk, to a design by Antonio Maggini of Italy, and it is very much in the style of 1970s fast Italian motor yacht. Mysteres were in production from 1975 to 1977, when they were superseded by the Mirage (illustrated), based on the same hull but with a new superstructure — still in the Italian style — and a new interior layout. Mirage remained in production until 1981, when JCL went into liquidation. A total of 43 Mysteres and Mirages were built.

The Mystere has four berths in two cabins, plus a settee-cum-double berth in the wheelhouse/saloon and (betraying her Italian origins) a single crew's berth in a tiny cabin under the foredeck. The Mirage has six berths in three cabins, plus the convertible double in the wheelhouse/saloon, and the crew's cabin forward.

Most Mysteres and Mirages were fitted with twin 210hp Ford Sabre diesels, giving top speeds of 25 to 26 knots. On the Mirage the engines were placed aft and worked through V-drives — hence the space for an extra cabin.

NELSON 44

Length overall	43ft 9in (13.34m)
Beam	13ft 0in (3.96m)
Draught	3ft 9in (1.14m)
Hull/deck material	GRP

THE Nelson 44 was designed specifically for Guernsey Boat Builders, who between 1977 and 1979 fitted out a dozen of the boats from a hull moulded by Robert Ives. Halmatic later took over the moulds and have built another 21 to date. Officially they call it the **Weymouth 44** (boats they fit out themselves) or the **Halmatic 44** (boats that other yards fit out), but most owners like to use the prestigious Nelson name, for this is another in the TT Boat Designs Nelson range of seaworthy semi-displacement motorboats.

Layout has always been very much to owners' requirements so the accommodation varies, but there are usually six or seven berths, with a large wheelhouse/saloon and small aft cockpit.

The most common engine installations are twin 212hp or 250hp Ford Sabre diesels, giving top speeds of about 20 and 22 knots.

INCHCAPE 45

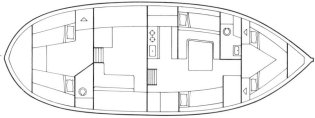

THE Inchcape 45 is one of a range of attractive and sturdy motor yachts and motor sailers designed on MFV (motor fishing vessel) lines by Francis Jones and James Evans, and built of larch on oak by Eyemouth Boat Building. The other boats in the range include the **inchcape 32** and the **Inchcape 38**, and there's also a 35-footer, of slightly finer lines, called the **Border Minstrel 35**. Altogether, Eyemouth Boat Building have built about 40 such boats since 1963, the 45 being the most popular.

The standard layout of the 45 has a large wheelhouse-cum-deck saloon just aft of amidships, with an aft cabin and a main saloon and forward cabin. But the exact layout of the accommodation varies from boat to boat. The number of berths varies from four to nine.

Power comes from a single diesel — typically a Gardner or Kelvin — of between 90 and 120hp, driving the boat at up to its maximum displacement speed of 8½ knots.

Length overall	45ft 0in (13.72m)
Beam	15ft 9in (4.80m)
Draught	5ft 9in (1.75m)
Hull/deck material	wood

NELSON 45

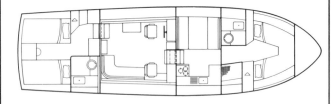

YET another boat in the famous TT Boat Designs Nelson range, this one was launched in 1972 and is still in production, 32 having been built to date, some as workboats and some as motor yachts. Tylers mould the hulls and various yards have fitted them out, including some of the cluster of boatbuilders in Bembridge, in the Isle of Wight, James & Caddy of Weymouth and, more recently, Seaward Marine of Guernsey. Most 45s have a wooden superstructure. A few are all GRP.

Interior layout varies from boat to boat, but usually includes a midships wheelhouse/saloon and an aft cabin, with as many as eight berths in all.

The Bembridge boats were fitted with twin 180 or 210hp Caterpillar diesels but later versions are mostly powered by two 212hp, 250hp or 300hp Ford Sabre diesels, giving top speeds from about 18 to 24 knots.

Length overall	45ft 0in (13.72m)
Beam	13ft 0in (3.96m)
Draught	3ft 6in (1.07m)
Hull/deck material	GRP or GRP/wood

Index

Boats in bold type

184

186

188

AUGUST 1991 £1.90

MOTOR BOATS MONTHLY

Radar: seven sets on test

Birchwood 39, Sea Star 23, Draco 34, Viking 58, Marex 27

Towing: what to do if the need arises

Win your ticket to Southampton

FOR THE NEXT 25 YEARS READ

MOTOR BOATS MONTHLY

BPL

Link House, Dingwall Avenue, Croydon, Surrey CR9 2TA
Telephone 081-686 2599 Telefax 081-781 6065

189